What is in Authentic Reading Practice?

The real world requires the use of many varied reading skills. Citizens
must be able to locate information, comprehend what is read, a...
act appropriately. Students must be taught the skills needed to...
food label, follow signage, assemble a toy, or gather informatio...
magazine article. *Authentic Reading Practice* provides this skill practice,
starting your students on their real-life reading adventure.

Using Authentic Reading Practice

- Each section may be used independently of the others.

- Teacher pages at the beginning of each section describe the activities
  and offer suggestions for their use.

- Introduce a skill with a guided lesson before asking students to practice
  independently. Reproducing the lessons on an overhead transparency will
  assist you in presenting a skill to the entire class.

- Assessment checklists are provided for each section. Use these to check
  specific behaviors observed, note special problems, and to plan lessons
  in areas of need.

- The models and practice pages presented in this book are only the
  beginning. When students understand a skill, provide additional practice
  using materials from real life.

Part 1

Reading Around the School

The activities in this section provide practice in reading the many kinds of environmental print that students encounter around the school.

Reading Labels

In order to feel comfortable and function smoothly in the classroom, students need to be able to read names for things they use and see every day. Fill your room with words and spend plenty of time "reading the room."

ACTIVITIES

Name It! (Pages 4 and 5)
Reproduce these pages to provide practice in attaching labels to items in the classroom.

Pick a Star (Pages 6 and 7)
Reproduce and cut out two sets of stars. Attach each star to the item it names. Place the second set of stars in a bag. Select one child at a time to pick a star from the bag and match it to one of the labels already placed in the room.

Books to Read (Page 8)
Place books in categories on your classroom library shelves. Label each area with labels you've laminated and cut apart.

"Things We Use" Bulletin Board (Page 9)
Set up a bulletin board containing real things students use at school. Label the items. Practice reading the board over a period of time. When you think your students are ready, take down the name labels. Show each label and select a student to pin it next to the correct item.

Reading Labels

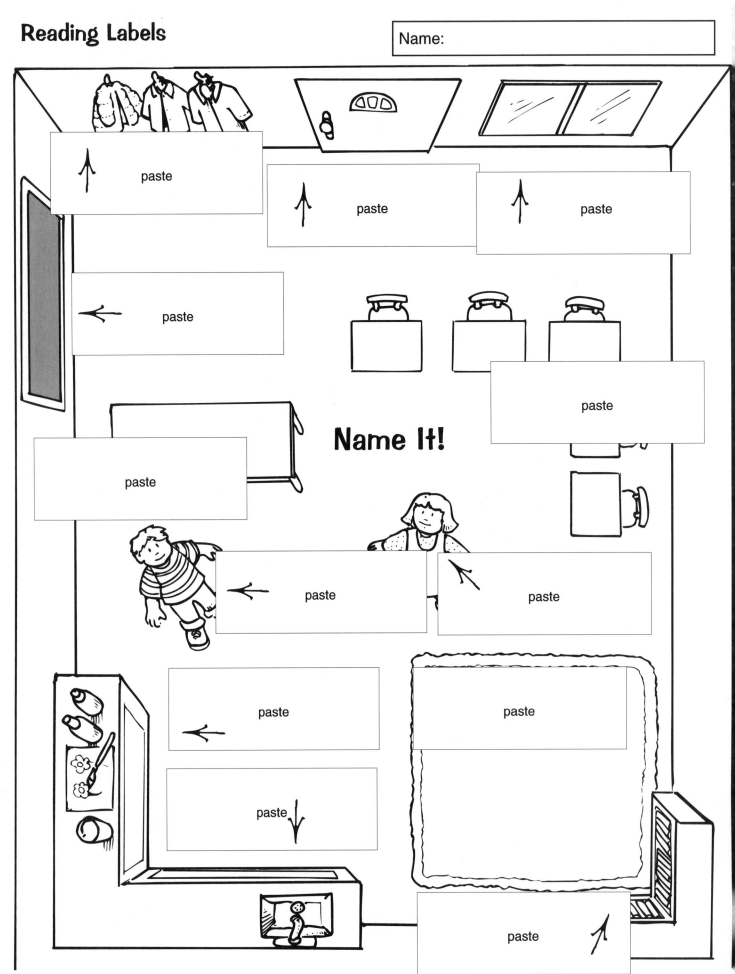

Name It!

Note: Reproduce this page and page 4 to use with "Name It!" on page 3.

Reading Labels

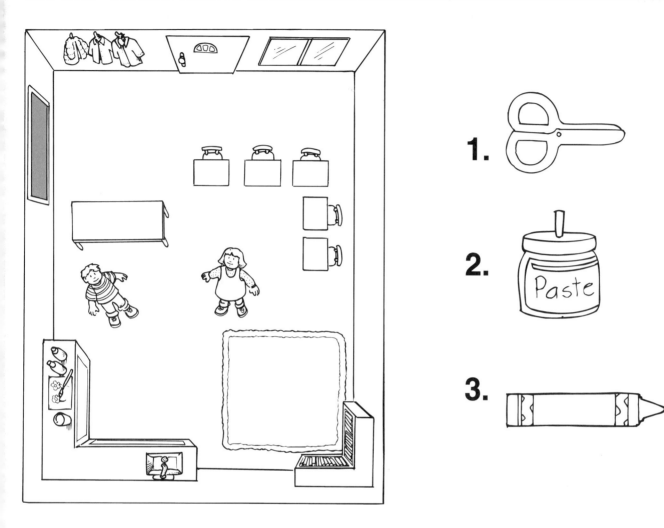

1.

2.

3.

coats	desks	sink
chalkboard	boy	rug
table	girl	books
door	paint	window

5

Reading Labels

paint

table

door

coats

chalkboard

paper

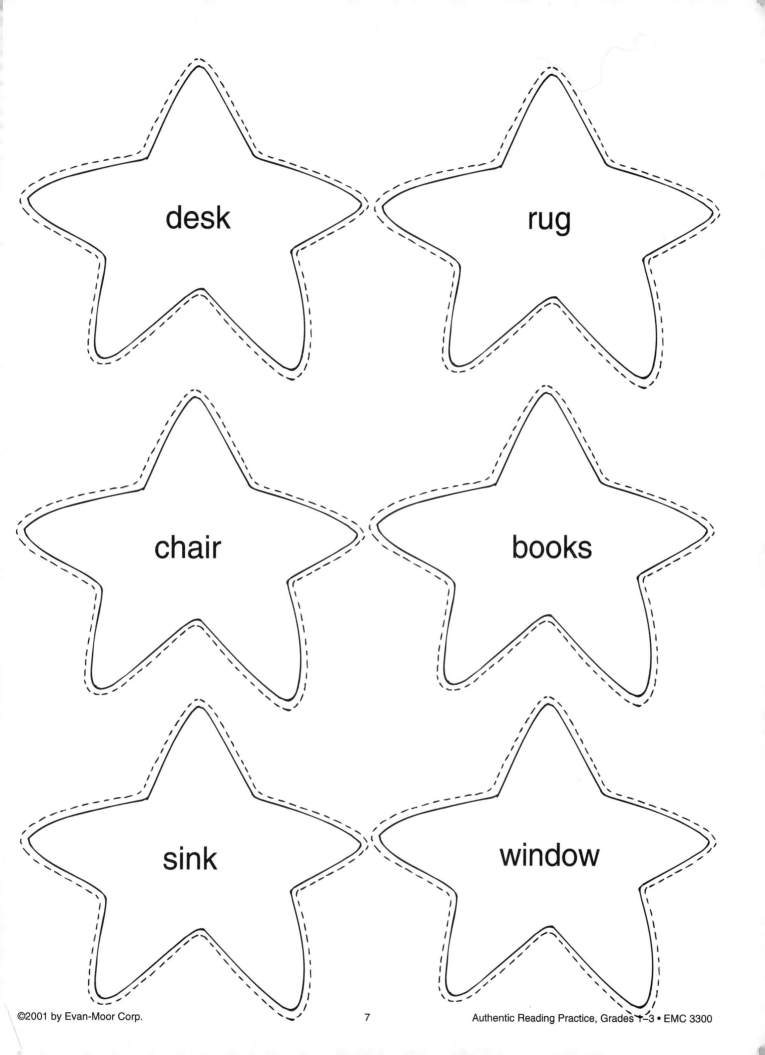

desk

rug

chair

books

sink

window

7

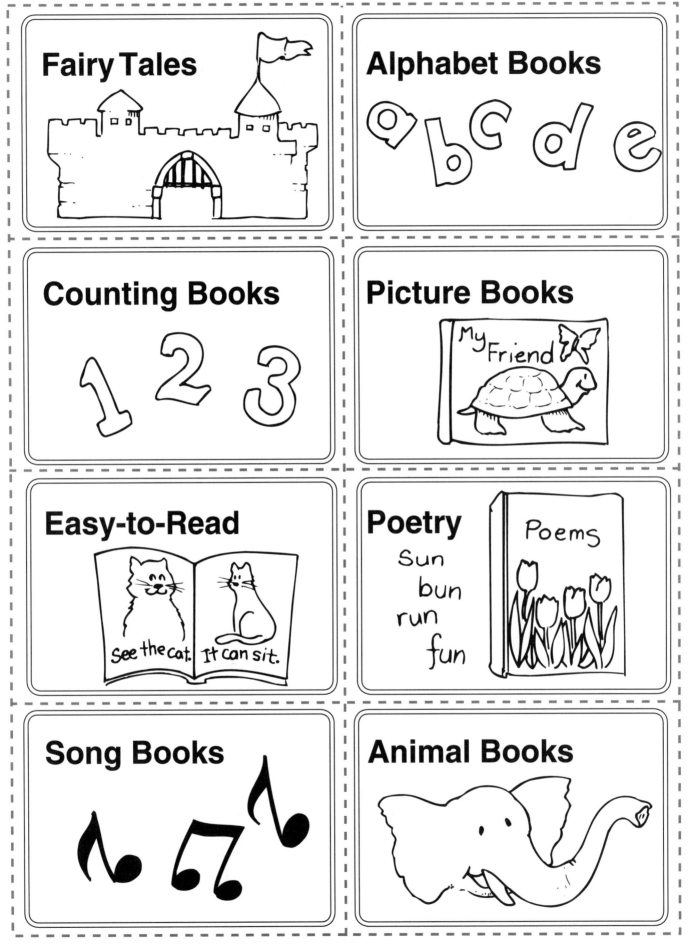

Fairy Tales

Alphabet Books

Counting Books

Picture Books

Easy-to-Read

See the cat. It can sit.

Poetry

Poems

Sun
bun
run
fun

Song Books

Animal Books

"Things We Use" Bulletin Board

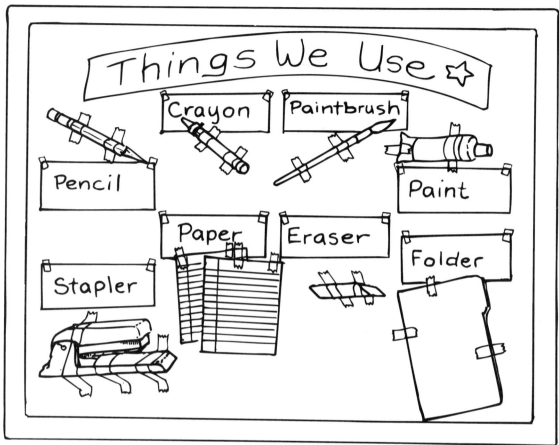

Materials
- butcher paper in two colors
- stapler
- marking pens
- pins or tacks
- cellophane tape
- real items that children use at school and home: pencil, pen, crayon, marking pen, paint, eraser, paper, paintbrush, folder, paper clip, etc.

Steps to Follow
1. Cover a large bulletin board with one color of butcher paper.

2. Cut a strip of butcher paper of a contrasting color. With a marking pen, write the title "Things We Use."

3. Attach real objects to the board.

4. Cut labels from contrasting butcher paper, write the names of the objects, and attach the labels to the board.

5. Ask students to read the name of each object as you point to it.

6. Repeat this over a period of time. When you think students are ready, take down the name labels. Show the labels one at a time and ask students to match each label to the object.

Reading Names

These activities make it fun for students to learn to read the names of the many people at school.

ACTIVITIES

Name Tags (Page 11)
Reproduce these name tags for students to wear at the beginning of the year, whenever there is a guest speaker or other visitors to class, and on field trips.

What's My Name? (Page 12)
Here are three activities that provide opportunities for students to read each other's names.

My Initials (Page 13)
You often want students to use initials when signing art projects. Here are some ways to make students aware of their initials.

My Name Hunt (Page 14)
Using the record sheet, students find someone in class whose first or last name begins with each letter on the sheet. That child writes the student's name on the line next to the letter.

Photo Bulletin Board (Page 15)
Use photos to help students learn to read the names of real people around the school.

My Very Own Spot (Page 16)
Reserve a spot for each student to display a favorite project. Let students take turns reading the names and hanging up each other's work.

Note: Reproduce these name tags whenever needed.

We are on a field trip!

My name is _____

Room: _____

School: _____

Hello!

My name is _____

What is your name? _____

Can we be friends?

I am a class helper.

My name is _____

My initials are

Authentic Reading Practice, Grades 1–3 • EMC 3300

What's My Name?

Name Lists Everywhere

Display lists of students' names in many locations:
- on a class helpers chart
- at centers
- on a birthday chart

Hop Along

You will need masking tape and 6″ (15 cm) square pieces of tagboard, one for each student.

Write a child's name on each card. Tape the cards to the floor in a grid or line. Have students hop from card to card, reading each name as they step on it.

We're in the Book

Create class books containing student names. These may be logs of field trips you've taken, photo books of your students at work in the classroom, or books in which students have drawn and written about themselves in the third person.

Tom and Sam like to paint.

My Initials

Use student names to practice identifying and naming letters.

1. Ask, "What letter does your first name begin with?" and "What letter does your last name begin with?" Explain that these are called your *initials*. Write a letter on the chalkboard and say, "Stand up if this letter is the initial of your first name." Repeat until you have covered all of the initials in your classroom.

2. Write your own name on the chalkboard. Underline the first letter in each of your names with colored chalk. Remind children that these letters are called *initials*. Call up several children at a time. Have them write their names on the board and underline their initials. Repeat until everyone has had a turn. Ask, "Does anyone in class have the same initials as you?"

3. Ask students to line up as you give the *first name* initials in ABC order. When everyone is in line, explain that they are lined up in the same order as the letters of the alphabet (alphabetical order).

4. Make a center activity by writing each person's initials and name on separate tagboard strips. Put five or more sets of names and initials in an envelope to use as a matching activity.

Name:

My Name Hunt

Look at the names of my friends.

B — — — — — — — — — — — — — — — — — —

K — — — — — — — — — — — — — — — — — —

S — — — — — — — — — — — — — — — — — —

W — — — — — — — — — — — — — — — — — —

T — — — — — — — — — — — — — — — — — —

R — — — — — — — — — — — — — — — — — —

C — — — — — — — — — — — — — — — — — —

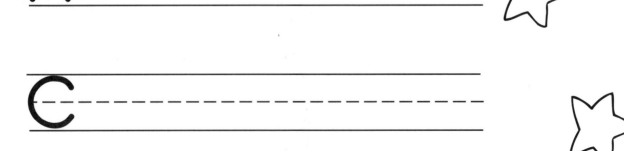

Photo Bulletin Board

Set aside a bulletin board for displaying photographs of real people around the school. List each person's name and job. Make reading the bulletin board part of "reading the room."

Who Am I?

Miss Peters
Principal

Mr. Polly
Custodian

Mr. John
Bus Driver

My Very Own Spot

Find a place in your classroom where each child can have a special spot to display a favorite project he or she has worked on. Let students change their work sample whenever they have a new one to share. The samples may be saved to add to the students' portfolio of work. The students' "Own Spot" may be reserved with clothespins and identification tags with their names on them.

Identification Tag Patterns

Authentic Reading Practice, Grades 1–3 • EMC 3300

Reading the Calendar

Your classroom calendar is a valuable instructional tool. These activities help students use the calendar to practice reading.

ACTIVITIES

A Class Log (Page 18)
Turn your calendar into a class log and provide another opportunity to begin reading words that are a part of daily life.

A Home Calendar (Page 19)
Reproduce this calendar each month for students to keep track of their schedule at home. Make one copy and write in the month, the dates, and special school events you want students and their families to remember.

Days of the Week (Page 20)
Reproduce, laminate, and cut apart the days of the week cards. Show the days in order and have students read them with you. Mix up the cards and show them one at a time. Have students read the word and select someone to show you that day of the week on the class calendar. Finally, place the cards in the chalk tray. Ask students to put them in the correct order. Depending on the experience level of your students, you may want to repeat this activity over time.

Months and Seasons (Pages 21 and 22)
Reproduce, laminate, and cut apart the months and seasons cards. Show the months in order and have students read them with you. Mix up the cards and show them one at a time. Have students read the word. Ask another student to find the name of the month that comes before or after. Let several students place the cards in order. Read the seasons cards. Hand a card to a student and ask him or her to pick the months cards that go with that season. Depending on the experience level of your students, you may want to repeat this activity over time.

A Class Log

Use a calendar log to keep a running record of the year's events.

Materials
- 42″ x 36″ (106.5 x 91 cm) butcher paper for each month
- wide-tip marking pen
- yardstick or meterstick
- monthly decorative items

Steps to Follow
1. Use a marking pen to divide the butcher paper as shown.

2. Write in the name of the month, days of the week, and dates.

3. Add monthly decorative items such as apples, pumpkins, hearts, etc. These may be purchased or made by students. (Each month you might assign a different group of students the task of decorating the class log.)

4. Take time before dismissal each day to review the day's events—something studied, a project undertaken, a special program or speaker, birthdays, a new student, etc.

5. Write what happened on the calendar log. Use words and/or pictures that your students can read. Review the information periodically throughout the month.

6. During the last week of school, post all the calendar logs to create a "time line" of what has happened in class for the year.

Note: Reproduce this page to use with "A Home Calendar" on page 17.

Name:	Month:	Sunday	Monday	Tuesday	Wednesday	Thursday	Friday	Saturday

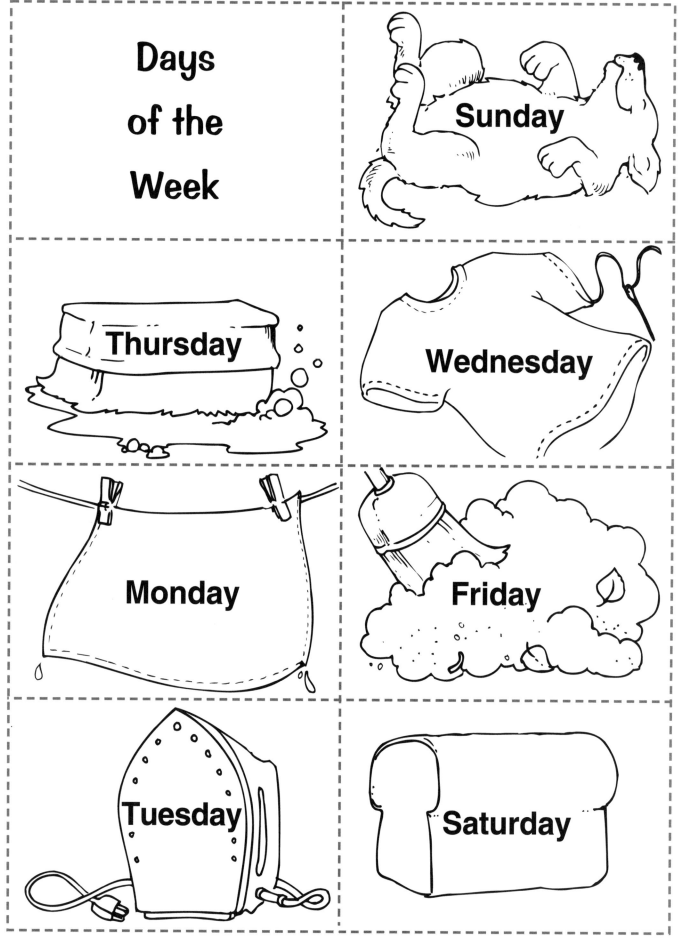

Days of the Week

Sunday

Thursday

Wednesday

Monday

Friday

Tuesday

Saturday

January	February
March	April
May	June
July	August

September	October
November	December
Winter	Spring
Summer	Fall

Words & Symbols That Give Directions

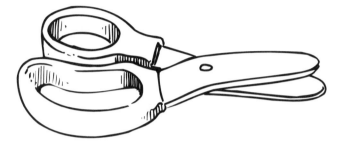

Students are constantly being asked to read words that tell them what to do. This section provides practice in learning those important words.

ACTIVITIES

Symbol Cards (Page 24)
Young students are helped by the use of symbols to indicate what they are to do. Show each symbol card and decide what action that symbol might indicate. Then place all the cards where students can see them. Ask questions that require students to choose a card. For example, "Which symbol would tell you to cut something out?"

Word Cards (Pages 25 and 26)
Reproduce the two pages of words that give directions. Read and discuss the meanings that are appropriate for your classroom. Practice with these cards over time until all students are comfortable reading the direction words. Add cards for other words that are particular to your classroom.

Words I Use Pop-up Book (Pages 27–29)
Everyone loves reading a pop-up book. This activity gives students further practice in reading the words and symbols they see every day. Make these books in small groups, giving directions at each step.

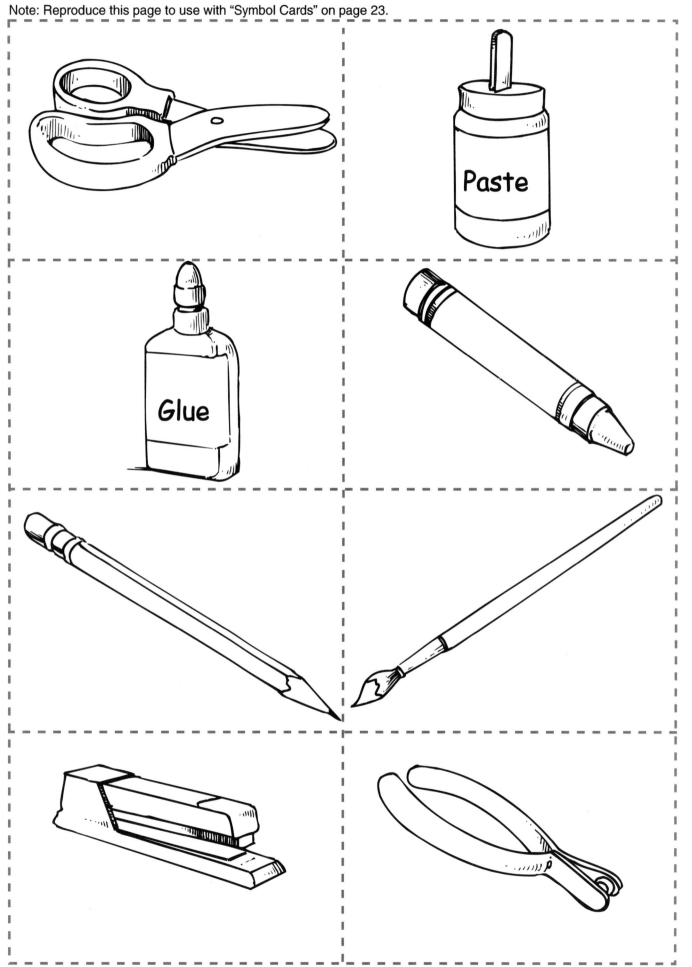

     24

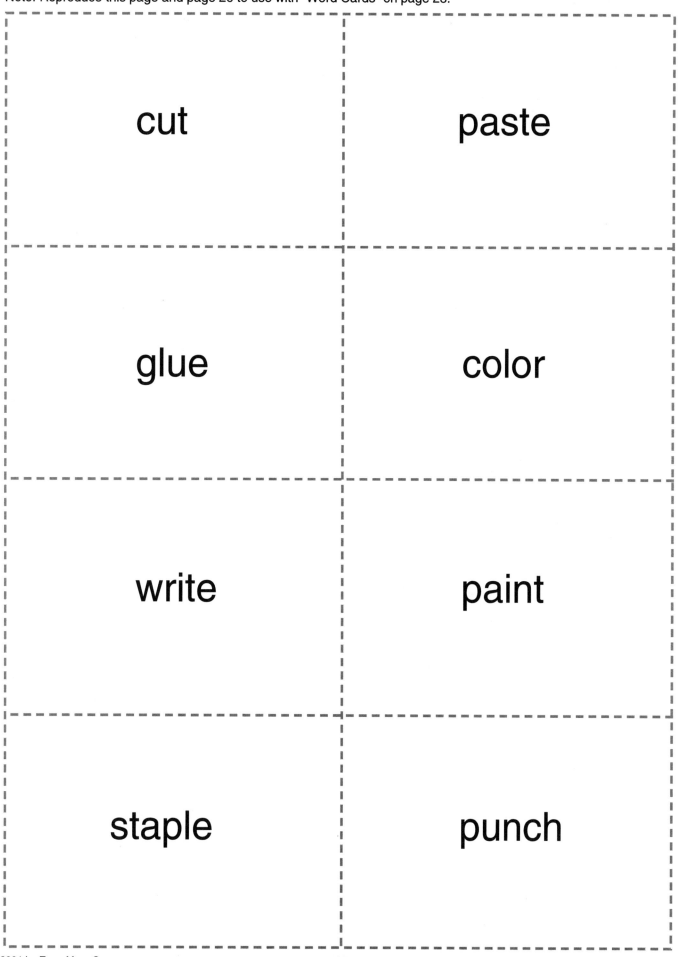

cut

paste

glue

color

write

paint

staple

punch

trace

fold

copy

underline

circle

match

draw

illustrate

Words I Use Pop-up Book

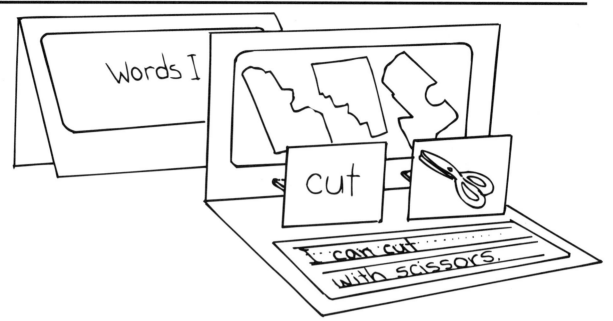

Materials
- pop-up form on page 28
- cover form on page 29
- copies of the cards on pages 24 and 25
- crayons, scissors, and paste

Steps to Follow
1. Cut and fold the pop-up form as shown by steps a through d.

2. Have each child choose one symbol card from page 24 and the matching word card from page 25.

3. Put paste on the front of each tab on the pop-up book. Affix the matching symbol cards on the tabs.

4. Write a phrase or sentence on the lines.

5. Color the background to show something about the sentence.

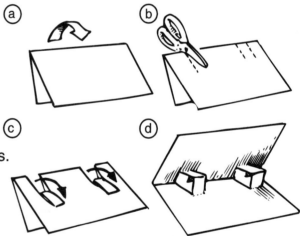

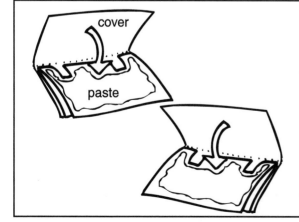

Put the pop-up in the cover:

Fold the cover form and place the closed pop-up form inside.

Smear paste on the top of the pop-up.

Close the cover and press.

Flip the book over and repeat the process.

Color the cover.

Authentic Reading Practice, Grades 1–3 • EMC 3300

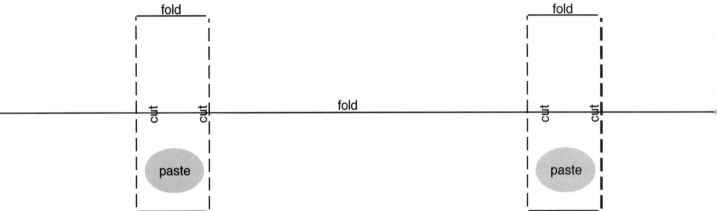

fold

fold

cut cut

cut cut

fold

paste

paste

The End

---

fold

Words I Use

Name

Reading Computer Vocabulary

The computer is an increasingly important teaching tool. These activities will help students read and use basic computer terms.

ACTIVITIES

Introduce Computer Terms (Page 31)
Follow these teacher directions to get students started reading computer terms such as *monitor, delete,* and *save.*

Computer Word Cards (Pages 31 and 32)
Reproduce the word cards on page 32 and follow the teacher directions on page 31 to practice reading computer vocabulary.

Make a Computer Terms Book (Pages 31–33)
Use the word cards on page 32 and the writing form on page 33 to make a class book.

Reading Computer Vocabulary

Introduce Computer Terms

1. Make a chart containing these terms:

computer	space bar	caps lock	save
monitor	enter	esc	keyboard
back space	page up	mouse	shift
printer	tab	delete	page down

2. Point to each term and read it for or with your students. Ask for a volunteer to explain what the term means or how the function is used. Provide an explanation for terms students don't know. Point to each word again and have the class read the chart.

3. Work with small groups at your computer keyboard. Have students point to and name each word that is listed on the chart.

Computer Word Cards

1. Reproduce the cards on page 32. (Make multiple sets so you have enough cards for one per student.) Pass out the cards. Have students read their cards. (Encourage them to help one another if they have difficulty.)

2. Give a definition of a term or function. The student who has that word card stands and reads it to the class. Collect the cards when all words have been covered.

3. Place the cards in a sack. Call on a student to draw a card from the sack. Have him or her read the card and explain the term.

Make a Computer Terms Book

1. Reproduce a copy of the form on page 33 for each student.

2. Pass out one computer word card on page 32 to each student. Students write their word in the box and then describe it.

3. Bind the completed pages in a construction paper cover. Use duplicates to create another copy of the book that can be loaned to other classes.

4. Select a student to draw a computer on the cover and add the title "Computer Terms."

computer	page up
space bar	mouse
caps lock	shift
monitor	page down
enter	printer
esc	delete
keyboard	tab
back space	save

Note: Reproduce this form to use with "Make a Computer Terms Book" on page 31.

Write word here

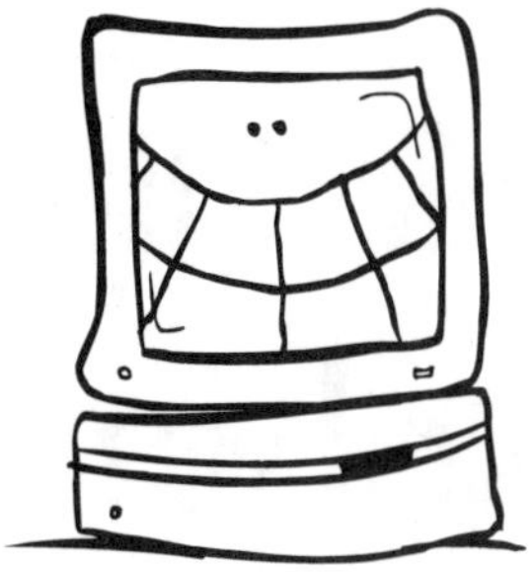

Write word here

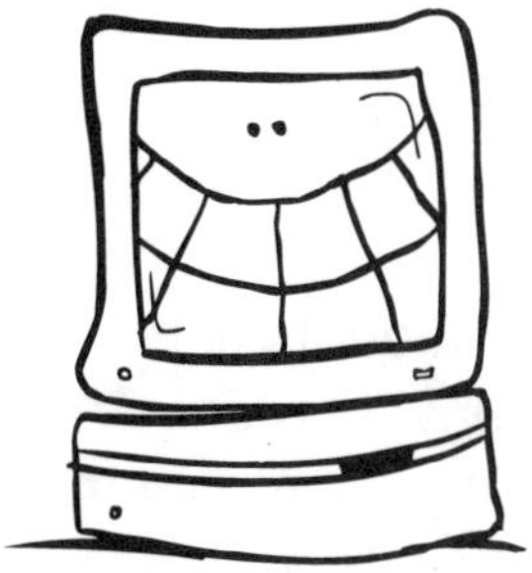

Signs Around the School & Neighborhood

Students need to learn to read common signs and symbols in their environment. These words and symbols are everywhere and provide important information about what to do, what not to do, where to go, and how to act safely.

ACTIVITIES

We're Going on a Sign Hunt (Page 35)
Take a walk around the school and the surrounding area to find signs.

School Places Word Cards (Pages 36 and 37)
Reproduce these cards that name places around the school. Practice them until students can read them easily. Be creative with games that will lend fun and variety to learning the words. Add other cards that name places specific to your site.

Signs and Symbols (Pages 38–43)
Follow the teacher directions on how to use the sign and symbol cards to help students learn to "read" important environmental print.

We're Going on a Sign Hunt

Individual clipboards on which to write the signs found during a sign hunt will keep students engaged in this activity.

Materials
- 6″ x 9″ (15 x 23 cm) piece of cardboard
- writing paper, cut slightly smaller than the cardboard
- hole punch
- string
- pencil
- stapler

Steps to Follow—Clipboard
1. Staple several sheets of writing paper to each piece of cardboard.

2. Punch a hole in the top right-hand corner of the board.

3. Attach a pencil with string.

Steps to Follow—Sign Hunt
1. As a class, walk around the school and surrounding area to find signs, warnings, and directions. Have students write what they find.

2. Share the results when you return to class. Compile a chart of all the "sign words" found.

3. Follow up by having students draw one of the places or signs and label the picture. Compile the drawings to create a class book entitled "Around Our School."

Note: Reproduce the cards on this page and page 37 to use with "School Places Word Cards" on page 34.

office	library
boys	girls
staff lounge	principal's office
nurse's office	cafeteria

multipurpose room	gymnasium
science lab	computer lab
music room	supply room
custodian's room	loading zone

Authentic Reading Practice, Grades 1–3 • EMC 3300

Signs and Symbols

Help ensure the safety and security of your students by teaching and practicing the recognition of important signs and symbols.

Materials
• cards on pages 39–43, reproduced, laminated, and cut apart or enlarged and made into overhead transparencies

Steps to Follow
1. Show each sign and ask, "What does this sign tell you?" Teach any words or symbols that are unfamiliar.

2. Practice using the signs and symbols in the following ways:

   • Mix up the cards. Show them one at a time and have a student name the symbol and explain what it tells us.

   • Sort the cards into two groups:

signs and symbols that warn us	signs and symbols that inform us

   • Use as sign and symbol riddles. Place the sign and symbol cards where students can see all of them. Give clues, such as the following, as to the identity of the symbols and allow students to pick out the symbol being described:

   > I don't want to put any of that in the punch!

   > We can cross the street now.

   > I can leave my aluminum cans at this location.

Note: Reproduce pages 39–43 to use with "Signs and Symbols" on page 38.

Authentic Reading Practice, Grades 1–3 • EMC 3300

Authentic Reading Practice, Grades 1–3 • EMC 3300

Authentic Reading Practice, Grades 1–3 • EMC 3300

Reading at Lunchtime

There's lots of motivation for students to learn to read words that are frequently used in the cafeteria.

ACTIVITIES

What's for Lunch? (Pages 45 and 46)
Take advantage of interest in the lunch menu to practice reading skills.

Lunch Lotto (Pages 47–49)
Play a game to reinforce the recognition of common "lunch" words.

What's for Lunch?

This lesson would be a terrific addition to your daily opening and calendar activities.

Materials
- page 46, reproduced on an overhead transparency, plus multiple copies
- ample supply of word cards, any size
- overhead projector

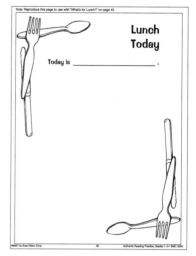

Steps to Follow
1. In advance, write the day's lunch menu on the overhead transparency and on a copy of page 46. Also make a word card for each item on the menu.

2. Read the menu on the overhead with the class.

3. Show each word card and read it together.

4. Pass the cards out to individual students.

5. Call out an item from the menu. The student holding that card brings it to the front and shows it to the class.

6. Repeat several times, passing the cards to different students.

7. Post the paper "Lunch Today" chart in a prominent place.

8. Conduct this activity daily to build a large menu-reading vocabulary. Review old word cards on a regular basis.

Lunch
Today

Today is _____ .

Lunch Lotto

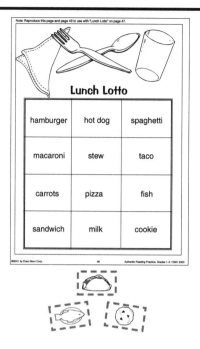

This game for four players is a fun way to practice mealtime vocabulary. Because the lotto cards have both words and pictures, the game can be played successfully by less able readers. When your students master the words given, white out the words on a copy of page 48 and create your own lotto game boards and cards to practice words from the school menu and students' own lunches.

Materials
- page 48, reproduced for each player
- 4 copies of page 49 for every 4 players—laminate for durability before cutting the cards apart

Steps to Follow
1. Each player takes a game card.
2. Shuffle the word cards and place them facedown in the center of the players.
3. Each player in turn draws a card, says the name of the food either by reading or naming the picture, and places the card on the matching spot of his or her game board. (If a player draws a duplicate card, it is placed in a discard pile and the player draws a new card.)
4. The first player to cover all the boxes on his or her game board is the winner.

Lunch Lotto

hamburger	hot dog	spaghetti
macaroni	stew	taco
carrots	pizza	fish
sandwich	milk	cookie

hamburger

hot dog

spaghetti

macaroni

stew

taco

carrots

pizza

fish

sandwich

milk

LOW FAT

cookie

More Opportunities to Read at School

Be watchful for every opportunity to bring print into your classroom environment. Students are highly motivated to read things that have to do with themselves and their experiences.

ACTIVITIES

Charts and Lists (Page 51)
Just about any classroom experience can be recorded on a chart to read.

Make a Class Scrapbook (Pages 52–54)
This record of class events will be one of the favorite books in your classroom library.

Charts and Lists

Songs We Sing
- Eensy Weensy Spider
- Farmer in the De[ll]
- Mary Had a Little Lamb
- Row Row Row Your Boat

Favorite Books

Strega Nona
Little White House
Sing a Song
Drummer Boy

Our Birthdays

[Jona]thon-January 10
[Mich]elle-June 16
[Mo]rgan-December 26

Post charts and lists for students to read. Some of these can stay up all year, while others will change as your curriculum and the seasons change.

1. Post charts with words and pictures for units of study. For example, if you are studying animals, make a chart of animal pictures with their names and a sentence or two describing each animal and what it does.

2. Post charts containing poems your students have learned and poems they have written.

3. Keep ongoing lists of the following:
   • songs they've learned
   • books you've read aloud
   • visitors to the class

4. Make a chart listing student birthdays. Charts and lists may be made on large sheets of tagboard, chart paper, or butcher paper. Write a heading and add a decorative illustration or border.

Make a Class Scrapbook

Keep an ongoing class scrapbook containing photographs and text about daily class activities, special events, guests, trips, letters, and other memorabilia collected for students to read. Read pages from the scrapbook periodically with your students. Place the scrapbook in the class library for everyone to read.

Materials
- a brown paper grocery bag (with or without an attached handle)
- butcher paper
- 4 large brass paper fasteners
- copies of page headings on pages 53 and 54
- hole punch
- tape or glue

Steps to Follow

1. Cut the brown paper grocery bag as shown:

Cut out the bottom.   Cut up the sides.

2. Cut sheets of butcher paper slightly smaller than the bag for the inside pages. Start with 18 sheets and add others as needed.

3. Punch holes in the two cover pieces and the inside pages.

4. Reproduce the labels on pages 53 and 54 to head various sections of the scrapbook.

5. Tape or glue pictures, photos, and other memorabilia to the inside pages. Label each item to help children remember its significance.

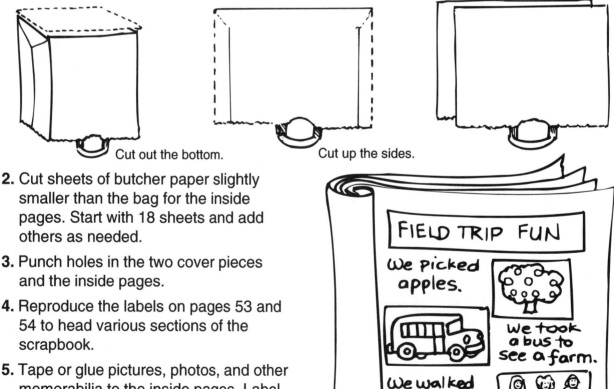

Here Is Our Class

Field Trip Fun

Visitors to Our Room

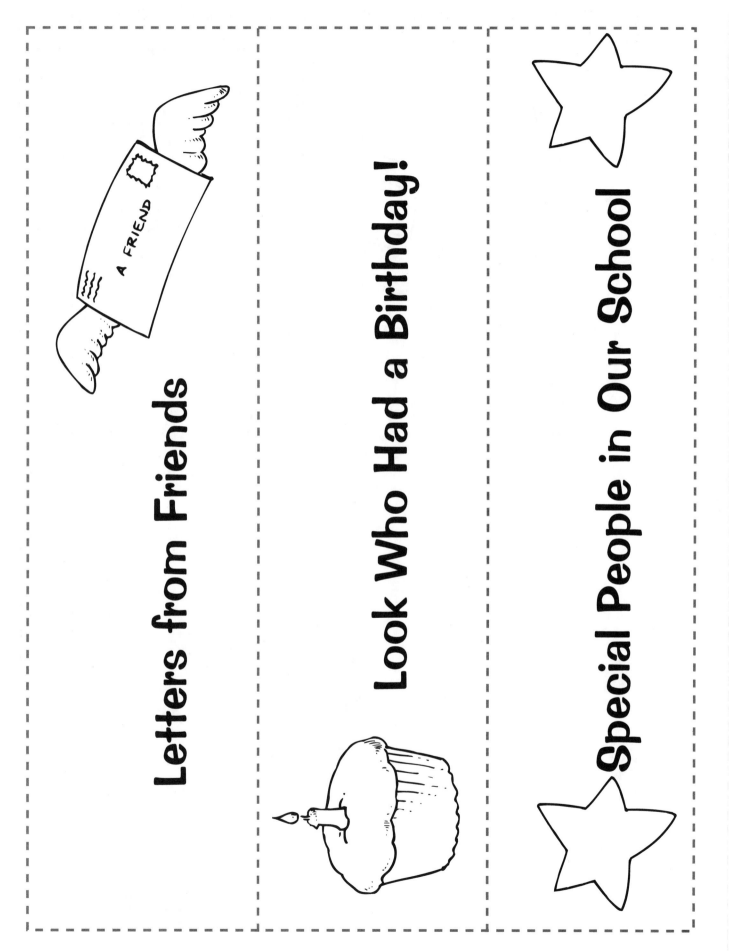

Letters from Friends

Look Who Had a Birthday!

Special People in Our School

Reading Around the School Skills Checklist ✓

	Students' Names									
Reads words and labels posted around the room										
Recognizes classmates' names in print										
Reads and writes own initials										
Recognizes the names of school workers										
Reads the names of the days of the week										
Reads the names of the months of the year										
Reads common words used in directions										
Reads common computer terms										
Reads the names of places around the school										
Recognizes common signs										
Reads words commonly used on school menus										

Parent News

Dear Parents,

Your child has been learning to read letters, names, symbols, signs, and words that appear in and around our school. You can help extend your child's language and reading skills using the things that are commonly read in and around your home.

1. Read to your child frequently. This helps your child develop a large vocabulary and increases his or her knowledge and understanding. In addition, it shows your child that you think reading is important.

2. Let your child see you read frequently. The material can be books, magazines, or the newspaper. Point out the times you read for information, such as following directions when you make something, locating a word in the dictionary, or looking up a telephone number. Again, you are demonstrating that reading is important and useful.

3. Use common items and everyday events to increase your child's vocabulary.

   • Help your child read street signs and signs on buildings in your neighborhood.

   • Point to letters in magazines and newspapers. Ask your child to name the letter and give its sound.

   • Use the newspaper or magazines to help your child practice reading words. Have him or her try to find and read words being learned at school.

   • Help your child learn to read the names of the members of your family and friends.

   • Help your child read the labels on packages and containers in the kitchen.

You are the most important teacher in your child's life. Your support will help your child continue to be a successful learner.

Sincerely,

Part 2

Reading to Follow Directions

The ability to read and follow directions accurately is a critical skill. The activities in this section provide students with practice in following both picture and written directions. Guided whole-class activities are followed by a series of center projects for independent practice.

Starting to Read Directions

Get your students thinking about how to follow directions with these introductory activities.

ACTIVITIES

Read and Do (Pages 59–61)
Reproduce the direction cards and glue them to tagboard for durability. Depending on the reading level of your students, either read each direction card to them or have them read independently. You may ask individuals or the whole class to perform each direction.

Follow the Directions (Page 62)
Reproduce the directions for individual students or read them aloud to the whole class. Students will need a sheet of blank paper, a pencil, and crayons.

More Practice with Directions (Pages 63 and 64)
Depending on the level of your students, these pages may be done together as a whole class or independently.

Note: Reproduce pages 59–61 to use with "Read and Do" on page 58.

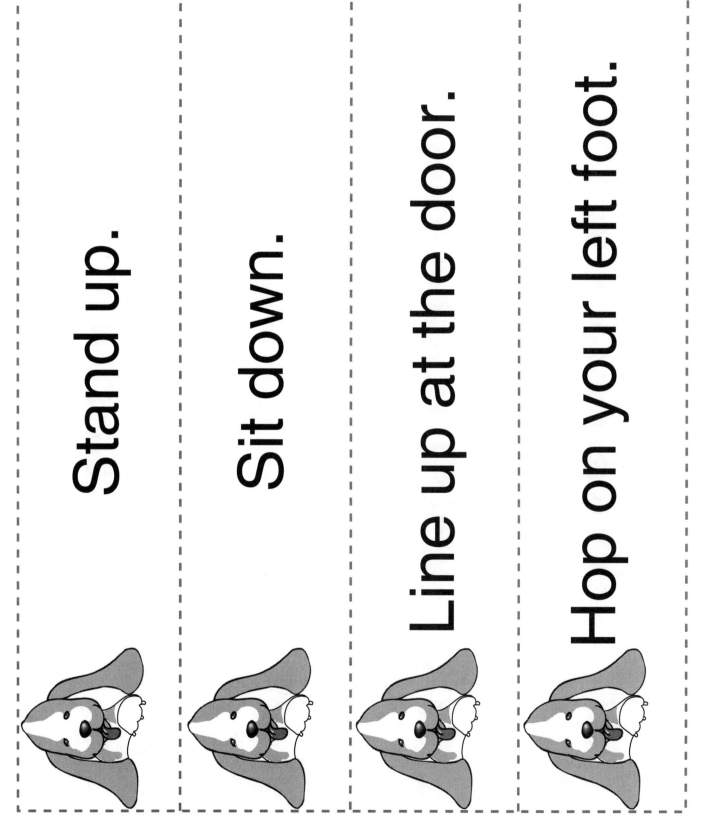

Stand up.

Sit down.

Line up at the door.

Hop on your left foot.

Authentic Reading Practice, Grades 1–3 • EMC 3300

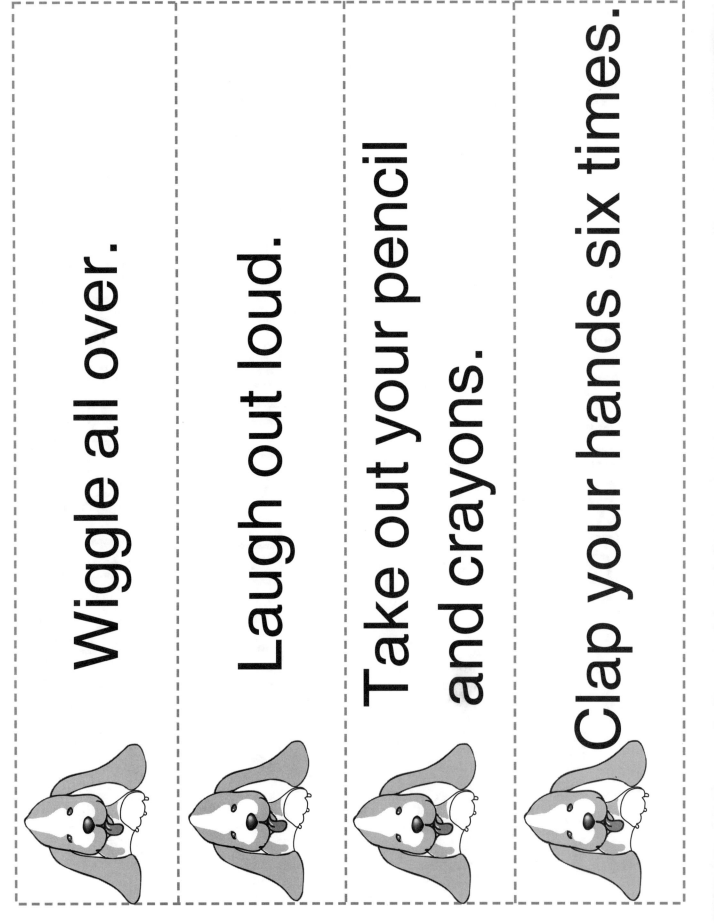

Wiggle all over.

Laugh out loud.

Take out your pencil and crayons.

Clap your hands six times.

Authentic Reading Practice, Grades 1–3 • EMC 3300

Set your chair on top of your desk.

Raise your hand if you can read this card.

Turn and shake hands with your neighbor.

Sit down and fold your hands in your lap.

Note: Reproduce this page to use with "Follow the Directions" on page 58.

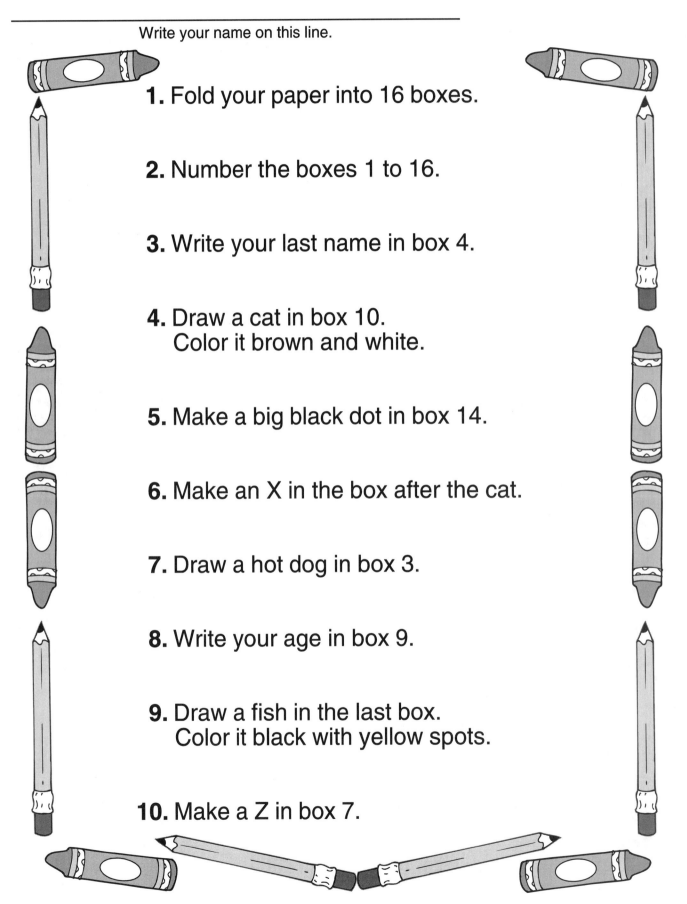

_____
Write your name on this line.

1. Fold your paper into 16 boxes.

2. Number the boxes 1 to 16.

3. Write your last name in box 4.

4. Draw a cat in box 10.
Color it brown and white.

5. Make a big black dot in box 14.

6. Make an X in the box after the cat.

7. Draw a hot dog in box 3.

8. Write your age in box 9.

9. Draw a fish in the last box.
Color it black with yellow spots.

10. Make a Z in box 7.

Name: _____

I Can Decide What to Do

Read the directions in each box and follow them.

Circle the answer.

I like dogs.

Yes   No

Draw a line under the cat.

Make an **X** on the boy.

Color the fish.

Follow the Instructions

Read the directions in each box and follow them.

1. Underline the taller animal.

2. Circle all of the color words.

red   green   fast

two   blue   pickle

3. Make an **X** on the last tree.

4. Make a check in front of six.

4   9   6

2   7   3

5. Draw a red car.

6. Write the words that rhyme.
clown   duck
house   flower
boat   brown

7. Describe the fruit.

8. Ask three children, "What do you like to play?" Write their answers.

1.

2.

3.

Reading Directions in School Subjects

Each school subject has special words and procedures that students must be able to read. The lessons in this section help students recognize what they must pay attention to when they read instructions in math, science, and art.

ACTIVITIES

Reading Directions in Math (Pages 66–69)
Page 66 provides teacher instructions for using the activities on pages 67–69.

Reading Directions in Science (Pages 70 and 71)
Page 70 provides teacher instructions for using the activity on page 71.

Reading Directions in Art (Pages 72–75)
Page 72 provides teacher instructions for using the activities on pages 73–75.

Reading Directions in Math

Teaching Strategies

• Reading math equations or word problems is like reading directions. They contain the clues to the procedures needed to solve the problems. Ask your students to analyze some problems.

What directions are in this equation? *(The problem tells us to add the first two numbers and then to subtract the last number.)*

$$6 + 2 - 3 =$$

What directions are in this word problem? *(The problem tells us to find how many birds were left. "Were left" is a clue that tells us to subtract.)*

8 birds were sitting on a fence. My cat chased 3 of the birds away. How many birds were left?

• Explain that before beginning ANY math lesson, you need to read all of the directions. If there is a word problem, read the problem carefully. If there are equations, read the signs carefully. Write the following steps on a chart and post it in class.

> When you do math problems
> 1. Read.
> 2. Think. What did it ask?
> 3. Do.
> 4. Read again.
> 5. Check your answer.

Practicing Strategies

Pages 67–69 contain sample problems at three levels of difficulty. Use any or all of these with your students to practice following directions.

1. Make transparencies of the pages you wish to use or reproduce them for each student.

2. Read the directions with your class. Discuss what each step says to do.

3. Go back to the first step. Read it as a group. Have students do just that much. Continue this process with each of the remaining steps.

4. Read each step once more as students check to see that they followed that step.

Find the Answer

Problem:

$2 + 8 - 5 =$

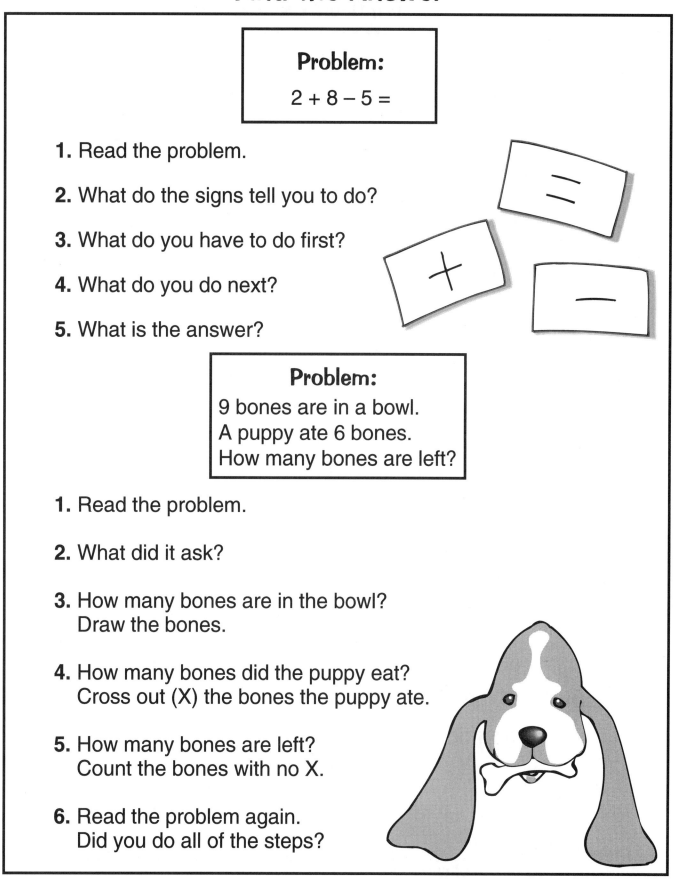

1. Read the problem.

2. What do the signs tell you to do?

3. What do you have to do first?

4. What do you do next?

5. What is the answer?

Problem:

9 bones are in a bowl.
A puppy ate 6 bones.
How many bones are left?

1. Read the problem.

2. What did it ask?

3. How many bones are in the bowl?
Draw the bones.

4. How many bones did the puppy eat?
Cross out (X) the bones the puppy ate.

5. How many bones are left?
Count the bones with no X.

6. Read the problem again.
Did you do all of the steps?

Bird Eggs

Problem:

Five birds each made a nest in the tree.
Two eggs are in each nest.
How many eggs are there in all?

1. Read the problem. What did it ask?

2. How many birds made nests?
Draw the nests.

3. How many eggs are in each nest?
Draw the eggs.

4. Count the eggs.
How many eggs are there in all?

5. Read the problem again.
Did you do all of the steps?

Bonus:
Can you think of two more ways
to find the answer?

Letters in Our Names

Problem:

With which letter of the alphabet
do the most names in class begin?

1. Write the letters of the alphabet in a row on the chalkboard.

2. Make a tally mark under the letter that each student's name starts with.

3. Count the tally marks for each letter. Write the numeral under the tally marks.

4. What is the answer to the problem?

5. Now answer these questions:

   How many names started with A?

   Did any names start with Z?

   How many names started with the same letter as your name?

H

J

I

W

V

X

Y

Z

N

S

T

U

R

Reading Directions in Science

Model the procedure for reading directions in science by doing the experiment on page 71 with your students.

1. Make a transparency of the directions on page 71 or reproduce the page for each group of students. Prepare a set of materials for each group conducting the experiment.

2. Divide the class into groups of four. Give each child in the group a number. Explain that child #1 will do the first step (collect needed materials). Child #2 will do step two, and so on. Everyone will help with cleanup.

3. Read the question to be answered by the experiment. Discuss what is being asked. Read the four possible answers. Have each group decide what they think will happen.

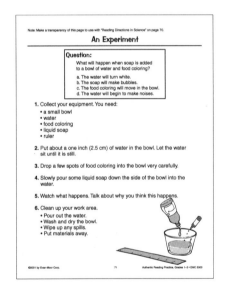

4. Read through the directions with your students. Discuss what is to be done at each step.

5. Go back to the first direction. Read it with your students and have child #1 in each group do the step.

6. Go on to the next direction. Call on child #2 to do that step. Continue until all directions have been completed. Record each group's results.

7. Go back through all of the steps to check that they were done. Discuss what might happen if you misread a direction or skipped one.

Note: Make a transparency of this page to use with "Reading Directions in Science" on page 70.

An Experiment

> ## Question:
>
> What will happen when soap is added to a bowl of water and food coloring?
>
> a. The water will turn white.
> b. The soap will make bubbles.
> c. The food coloring will move in the bowl.
> d. The water will begin to make noises.

1. Collect your equipment. You need:

- a small bowl
- water
- food coloring
- liquid soap
- ruler

2. Put about a one inch (2.5 cm) of water in the bowl. Let the water sit until it is still.

3. Drop a few spots of food coloring into the bowl very carefully.

4. Slowly pour some liquid soap down the side of the bowl into the water.

5. Watch what happens. Talk about why you think this happens.

6. Clean up your work area.

- Pour out the water.
- Wash and dry the bowl.
- Wipe up any spills.
- Put materials away.

Reading Directions in Art

If you instruct your students in reading directions to complete an art project, the possibilities for independent projects expand tremendously.

Make a Stamp for Printing

Materials
- scissors
- glue
- pencil
- plastic bottle cap
- stamp pad

- scratch paper—3″ (7.5 cm) square
- foam shoe inner sole—3″ (7.5 cm) square
- cardboard—4″ (10 cm) square
- construction paper—6″ x 9″ (15 x 23 cm)
- page 73, reproduced on an overhead transparency or for each student

Steps to Follow
1. Read all of the directions as a group. Discuss the meaning of terms such as *design, inner sole,* and *handle.*

2. Do each step one at a time as students create a simple design and make a stamp.

3. Use the completed stamp to make patterns on construction paper. (The stamps may also be used to make stationery or greeting cards.)

Read and Draw

Materials
- cards on page 74, reproduced, glued to tagboard, laminated, and cut out
- blank cards (use large file cards)
- drawing paper
- pencils, crayons, and/or marking pens

Steps to Follow
1. Pick the drawing directions from one card to write on the chalkboard for the entire class to follow.

2. Place the cards and drawing materials in a center for independent practice. Encourage students to use the blank cards to write drawing directions for classmates to follow.

Drawing Challenges

Page 75 provides three drawing challenges to add to the drawing center. Enlarge each challenge, and then mount them on tagboard, laminate, and cut apart.

Note: Make a transparency of this page to use with "Make a Stamp for Printing" on page 72.

Make a Stamp for Printing

Materials
- scratch paper
- inner sole
- cardboard
- plastic bottle cap
- construction paper
- stamp pad
- pencil or black marking pen
- glue
- scissors

Steps to Follow

1. Plan your design. Sketch it on scratch paper. Cut out the pattern.

2. Lay your design on the inner sole. Trace around the design.

3. Cut out the design.

4. Glue the design to the cardboard. Write your name on the other side of the cardboard.

5. Glue the bottle cap to the side with your name. This is a handle to help as you make a print.

6. Let the glue dry.

7. Press the stamp on the stamp pad. Make a pattern on the construction paper.

Read and Draw

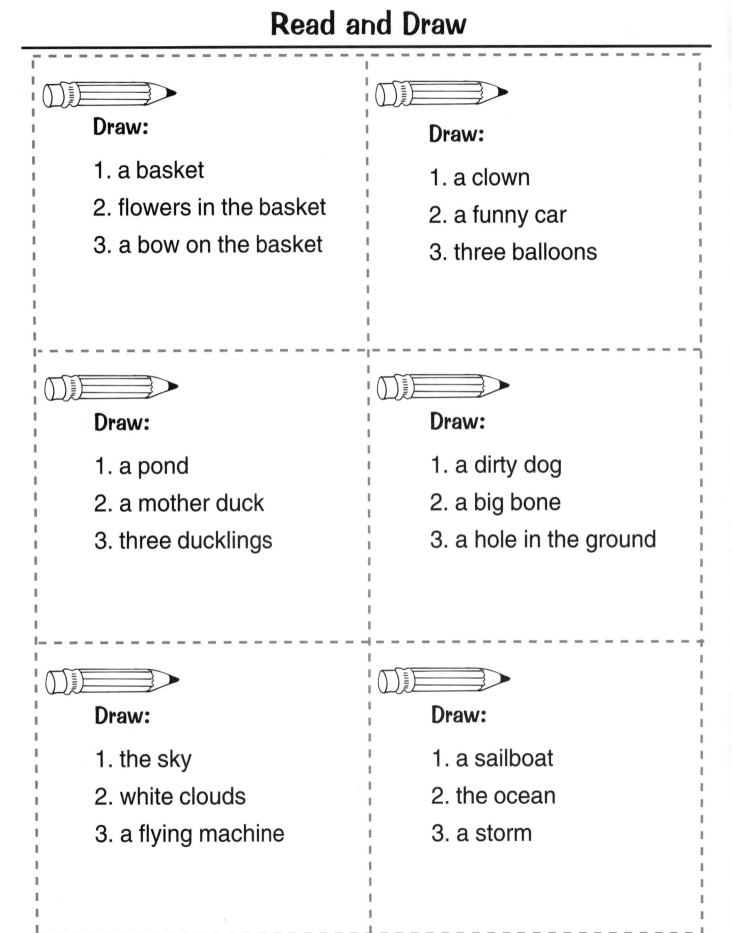

Draw:

1. a basket

2. flowers in the basket

3. a bow on the basket

Draw:

1. a clown

2. a funny car

3. three balloons

Draw:

1. a pond

2. a mother duck

3. three ducklings

Draw:

1. a dirty dog

2. a big bone

3. a hole in the ground

Draw:

1. the sky

2. white clouds

3. a flying machine

Draw:

1. a sailboat

2. the ocean

3. a storm

Note: Reproduce this page to use with "Drawing Challenges" on page 72.

Drawing Challenges

Think about how to draw a **mouse.**

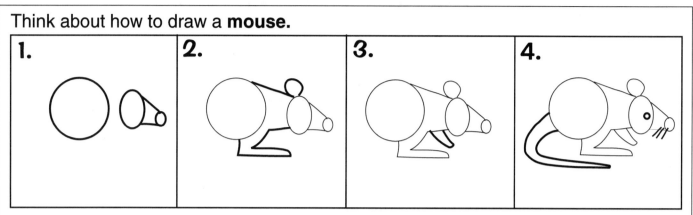

1.   **2.**   **3.**   **4.**

Drawing Challenge:

Draw a mother mouse with three babies.
Show them in a nest in the forest.

Think about how a **frog** looks when it is sitting.

1.   **2.**   **3.**   **4.**

Drawing Challenge:

Draw a frog sitting on a log.
Show the frog catching a bug to eat.

Think about how to draw a **dragon.**

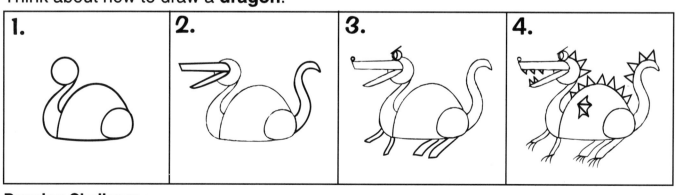

1.   **2.**   **3.**   **4.**

Drawing Challenge:

Draw a big green dragon.
Show fire and smoke coming out of its nose.

Reading Directions to Cook

This section introduces cooking terms and provides some simple cooking experiences that allow students to practice reading special cooking vocabulary.

ACTIVITIES

Cooking Terms (Page 77)
Cooking has a vocabulary of its own. There are special names for equipment, procedures, and measurement. Introduce these terms before beginning any cooking experiences.

Before You Cook (Pages 78 and 79)
Get used to cooking instructions by reading package preparation instructions and acting out group cooking reminders.

Let's Cook (Pages 80–82)
Teacher hints and three simple recipes to get your room cookin'!

Cooking at Home (Page 83)
Send home this letter and cooking form, asking parents to supervise as their child reads directions and cooks something. When students return the form, provide time for sharing what they made and describing the steps they followed.

Cooking Terms

Cooking has a vocabulary of its own. There are special names for equipment, procedures, and measurements. Introduce these terms before beginning any cooking experiences.

Materials
- chart paper
- marking pen
- real cooking items—measuring spoons and cups, bowls, utensils, etc.
- large file cards
- pencils and crayons

Steps to Follow

1. Brainstorm to make a list of cooking terms students already know. Record these under headings on chart paper as shown below. Add new terms as they are learned.

2. Set up a display of real items labeled with their names. Point to each item and have students give its name and describe its use.

3. Make a matching game using cooking terms to provide ongoing practice in reading cooking terms.

   - Give each student a file card and assign one cooking term.

   - Students are to fold the card in half, write the term on one half of the card, and illustrate the word on the other half.

   - Cut the cards in half and place them in a box. Place the box in a center for independent matching practice.

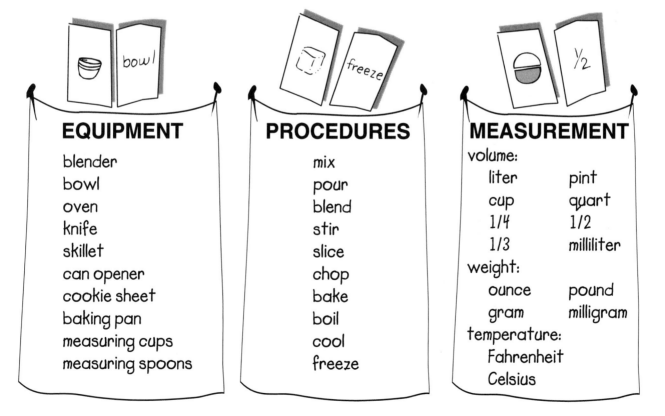

EQUIPMENT
blender
bowl
oven
knife
skillet
can opener
cookie sheet
baking pan
measuring cups
measuring spoons

PROCEDURES
mix
pour
blend
stir
slice
chop
bake
boil
cool
freeze

MEASUREMENT
volume:
    liter   pint
    cup   quart
    1/4   1/2
    1/3   milliliter
weight:
    ounce   pound
    gram   milligram
temperature:
    Fahrenheit
    Celsius

Before You Cook

Reading Cooking Directions on Packages

• Bring in an assortment of packages containing preparation instructions. Instant pudding, microwave popcorn, instant soup, muffins, etc., all have fairly simple instructions. Ask parents to send in empty boxes and you'll have a nearly endless supply.

• Divide the class into groups. Have each group read the directions on one or two packages. Each group will then present their item(s) to the class and explain how the product is to be prepared.

• Place the containers in an accessible spot for students to practice reading on their own.

Act It Out

Before doing any formal cooking experiences, practice procedures students must follow.

Materials
• hand soap
• paper towels
• apron
• ingredients—raisins, banana chips, chocolate chips, peanuts*
• utensils—paper muffin cups, tablespoon, stir sticks
• chart paper
• page 79, reproduced on an overhead transparency

Steps to Follow
1. Set out the ingredients, utensils, etc.

2. Divide the class into small groups.

3. Read all the directions on the transparency together.

4. Reread the directions one at a time. Choose a student from each group to act out the step. Evaluate the execution of each instruction.

*Make sure no one is allergic to peanuts.

Instructions for Cooking

1. Wash your hands carefully.

2. Put on an apron.

3. Collect your ingredients from the food table.

4. Collect your utensils from the equipment table.

5. Read the recipe with your group.

6. Decide who is going to do each step.

7. Take the completed food to the serving table.

8. Clean up your work area.

Trail Mix

How to make:
- Place in a muffin cup:
  1 tablespoon raisins
  1 tablespoon banana chips
  1 tablespoon chocolate chips
  1 tablespoon peanuts
- Mix with a stir stick.

Utensils:
muffin cup
tablespoon
stir stick

Let's Cook

Some Guidelines

1. Have students work in small groups with an adult helper when they cook.

2. Before the cooking experience, teach the use of necessary equipment (plastic knives only) and how to mix and measure ingredients.

3. Have each group prepare the same recipe or have each group prepare a different recipe, making enough for the whole class.

4. Discuss how to divide the tasks among the members of a group. One way would be to assign one person to each of these tasks—collect the materials, read the recipe, mix the ingredients, divide the servings.

Making Packaged Foods

Packaged mixes work well for small groups, and many may be put in a center for independent cooking experiences.

Muffins

For example, students might make muffins from a mix. You will need to provide:

toaster oven	mixing bowl
muffin tins	eggs
mixing spoon	water
package of muffin mix	

Adult help may be needed to ensure that the directions are read correctly. An adult needs to be responsible for putting the muffins in the oven and removing them.

Cooking from Scratch

Make a collection of simple recipes to use for classroom cooking.
• There are many excellent recipe books for children.
• Collect recipes that relate to a unit of work or a piece of literature you plan to share— churned butter, johnny cakes, Hoppin' John, etc.

Three simple recipes are provided on pages 81 and 82.

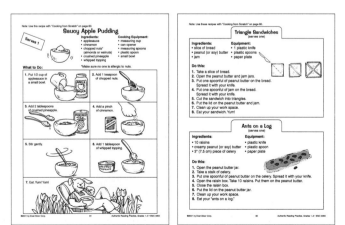

Note: Use this recipe with "Cooking from Scratch" on page 80.

Saucy Apple Pudding

Serves 1

Ingredients:
- applesauce
- cinnamon
- chopped nuts*
  (almonds or walnuts)
- crushed pineapple
- whipped topping

Cooking Equipment:
- measuring cup
- can opener
- measuring spoons
- plastic spoon
- small bowl

What to Do:

*Make sure no one is allergic to nuts.

1. Put 1/2 cup of applesauce in a small bowl.

2. Add 1 teaspoon of chopped nuts.

3. Add 2 tablespoons of crushed pineapple.

4. Add a pinch of cinnamon.

5. Stir gently.

6. Add 1 tablespoon of whipped topping.

7. Eat. Yum! Yum!

Authentic Reading Practice, Grades 1–3 • EMC 3300

Note: Use these recipes with "Cooking from Scratch" on page 80.

Triangle Sandwiches
(serves one)

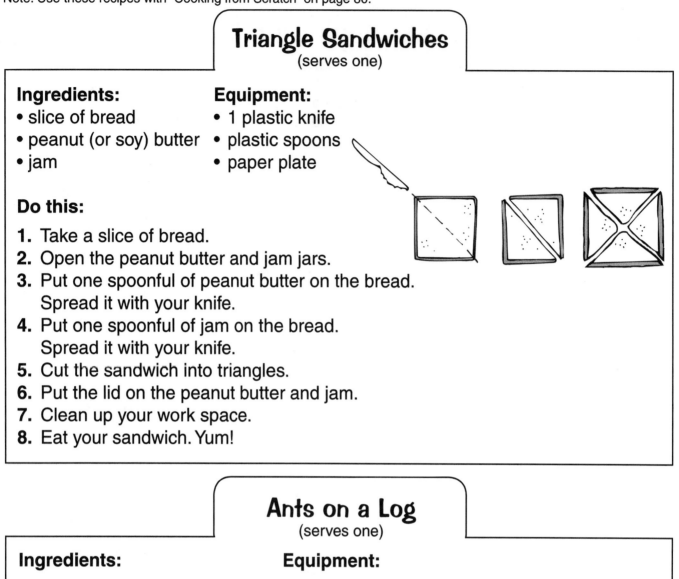

Ingredients:
- slice of bread
- peanut (or soy) butter
- jam

Equipment:
- 1 plastic knife
- plastic spoons
- paper plate

Do this:

1. Take a slice of bread.
2. Open the peanut butter and jam jars.
3. Put one spoonful of peanut butter on the bread. Spread it with your knife.
4. Put one spoonful of jam on the bread. Spread it with your knife.
5. Cut the sandwich into triangles.
6. Put the lid on the peanut butter and jam.
7. Clean up your work space.
8. Eat your sandwich. Yum!

Ants on a Log
(serves one)

Ingredients:
- 10 raisins
- creamy peanut (or soy) butter
- 3" (7.5 cm) piece of celery

Equipment:
- plastic knife
- plastic spoon
- paper plate

Do this:

1. Open the peanut butter jar.
2. Take a stalk of celery.
3. Put one spoonful of peanut butter on the celery. Spread it with your knife.
4. Open the raisin box. Take 10 raisins. Put them on the peanut butter.
5. Close the raisin box.
6. Put the lid on the peanut butter jar.
7. Clean up your work space.
8. Eat your "ants on a log."

Note: Reproduce this letter and record sheet to use with "Cooking at Home" on page 76.

Dear Parents,

At school we are practicing reading different types of directions. Preparing food is an excellent opportunity to read directions.

Please supervise as your child prepares a simple food item. This can be a snack or part of a meal. If necessary, help your child read any directions on the package or in the recipe.

Thank you for your help.

Return this form to school by _____ .

Date

- -

Name: _____

I Cooked at Home

I prepared:

_____

_____

I used these ingredients:

_____

_____

_____

This is how I made it:

_____

_____

_____

_____

It tasted:

_____

Draw a picture of the food you prepared on the back of this page.

Reading Directions at Home

The activities in this section will help students understand that there are directions to follow in places other than school, making the connection between classroom learning and real life.

ACTIVITIES

A Directions Hunt (Page 85)
As a class, brainstorm and list things at home that have directions. Make the list more "readable" for beginning readers by attaching pictures.
• Find pictures in magazines or catalogs.
• Draw pictures.
• Attach the real thing.

Using page 85, have pairs of students read the directions together.

I Can Read Directions to Do My Chores (Page 86)
Many children have regular chores to do at home. Help them to be aware that they follow directions to do these chores. Reproduce page 86 to be completed at home.

Do You Follow Directions? (Page 87)
Reproduce the form on page 87. Have students interview three people, asking the question, "What directions did you have to read today?" Have students record the answers on their forms. When the forms are returned to school, make a tally chart showing the answers. Compare how often various types of directions were read.

Name:

A Directions Hunt

Read the directions on each of these things.

Draw a box around the things you have at home.

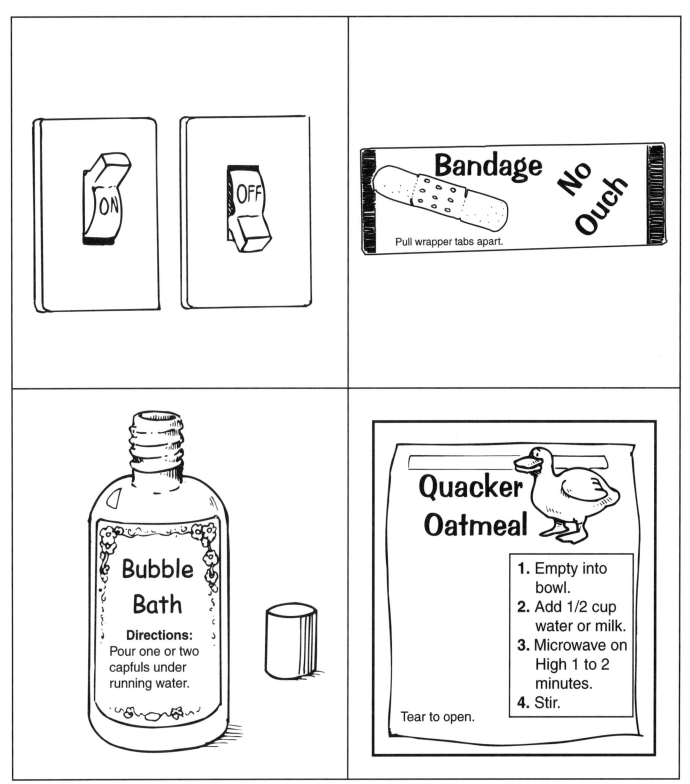

Dear Parents,

Many families have a set of chores that each family member is expected to do. A How-To Manual for doing chores clarifies these expectations. Have your child tell you the directions for one of the chores she/he is expected to do at home. Please write the directions on the lines below. Send the directions back to school so that we can practice reading them.

Thank you,

Name:

I Can Read Directions to Do My Chores

Parent:
Tell your parent the directions for doing one of the chores you do at home.

_____

_____

_____

_____

_____

_____

_____

_____

Draw yourself following the directions.

Name:

Do You Follow Directions?

Interview three people.
Ask, "What directions did you have to read today?"
Write their answers here.

1. _____
   name

2. _____
   name

3. _____
   name

Reading Directions to Put Things Together

"Some assembly required." Does that phrase horrify you? Reading directions to put something together is something many of us avoid. Let's help students be more comfortable with this skill by practicing it frequently and making it fun.

ACTIVITIES

Assembling Things (Pages 89 and 90)
Here are some teaching suggestions and a paper building activity to get students started with reading directions to put things together.

Assembling Things

Materials
- pictures or samples of things that have to be put together
- an object that requires simple assembly, with the directions reproduced on an overhead transparency
- page 90, reproduced for students

Steps to Follow

1. Show some things that have to be put together—a model airplane or car, a doll house, pattern pieces for making a clothing item, a toy, etc. Explain what parts had to be put together in these samples.

2. Discuss the types of things students and/or their parents have put together. Ask how they knew what to do. Invite students to bring something they have put together to share with the class.

3. Bring in an object that requires simple assembly. Gather the necessary tools.

4. Display the overhead transparency of the directions so that the class may help read them. Enlist student help in assembling the object.

5. Have students do page 90 for additional practice in reading instructions to put something together.

6. Set up an assembly center. Provide building toys— Legos®, Lincoln Logs®, etc. Create task cards that give directions for building specific structures. As students gain competence, let them write additional task cards for others to use.

Build a House

1. Cut out the rectangle.
2. Fold it 4 times.
3. Open it up. Cut on the dotted lines.
4. Fold and tape the roof. Do both ends.
5. Fold and tape both sides of the house.
6. Cut a door and fold it open.

Note: Reproduce this page to use with "Assembling Things" on page 89.

Build a House

1. Cut out the rectangle.

2. Fold it 4 times.

3. Open it up. Cut on the dotted lines.

4. Fold and tape the roof. Do both ends.

5. Fold and tape both sides of the house.

6. Cut a door and fold it open.

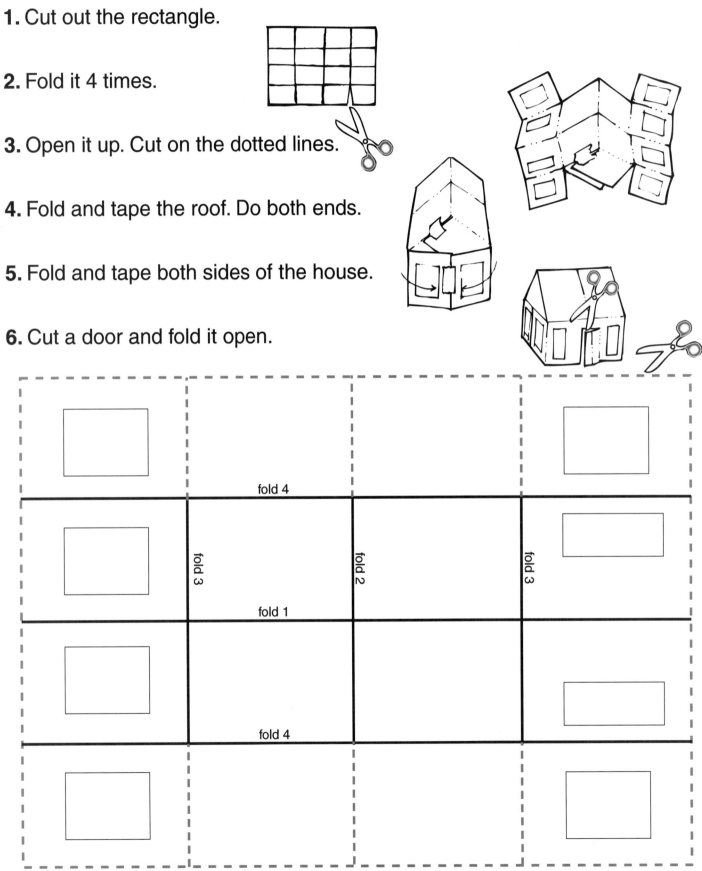

Writing Directions

Draw a Cat
1. Make a big circle for the body.
2. Make a small circle for the head.
3.
4.

As your students gain competence with reading directions, require them to write directions as well. This requires great attention to detail and sequence.

ACTIVITIES

How Do We Do It? (Page 92)
This activity will point out how detailed one must be when writing directions.

How Do You Cook It? (Page 93)
After a class cooking experience (see pages 76–83), have students write about the steps they followed to make the food.

How Do You Play It? (Page 94)
Have students write the instructions for playing a favorite game. Before they begin, brainstorm to make a list of things to include (number of players, equipment, rules, keeping score). When finished, pair students to read and revise their directions.

A How-to Manual for Your Classroom (Pages 95 and 96)
You spend a lot of time teaching procedures for your classroom. Create a classroom procedures reference manual and practice writing directions at the same time.

How Do We Do It?

Students often overlook the most obvious steps when writing directions. Group practice on a regular basis will help students become more methodical in their approach to writing directions.

1. Give one or more students a simple direction, such as:
   • Use your pencil to draw this cat on your paper.
   • Take out a book and read it.
   • Put on your jacket.
   • Go sharpen your pencil.

2. Ask the class to tell you the steps that they followed. Write these on the chalkboard or chart paper exactly as they tell you. Do not edit at this point.

draw the cat
get a book
sharpen pencil
put on a jacket

3. When the directions are completed, read them together to see what revisions are needed. Continue reading and revising until everyone agrees that the directions are clear.

Note: Reproduce this form to use with "How Do You Cook It?" on page 91.

Name:

How Do You Cook It?

How to Make ______________________________

recipe name

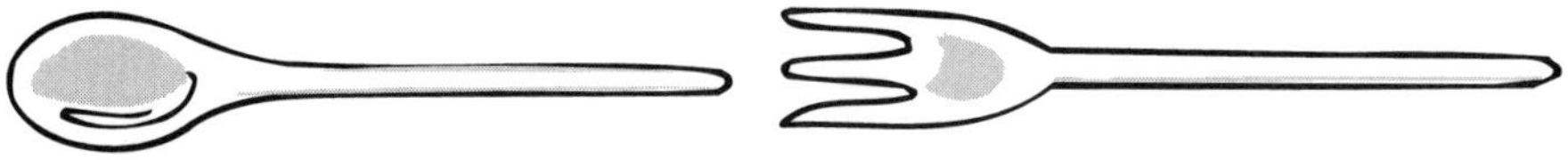

Get these ingredients:

____

____

____

____

Draw the finished food here.

Get this equipment:

____

____

____

____

Do this:

____

____

____

____

____

____

Note: Reproduce this form to use with "How Do You Play It?" on page 91.

Name:

How Do You Play It?

How to Play _____

game name

Number of Players _____

Equipment

Draw the game here.

_____

_____

_____

_____

Keeping Score

_____

_____

_____

_____

How to Play

_____

_____

_____

_____

_____

A How-to Manual for Your Classroom

Your students are familiar with the procedures you use daily. These classroom routines are ideal for practice in writing directions. You might write up one procedure each week until the manual is complete. Students will be proud that they have contributed to a manual that will help substitute teachers and visitors become acquainted with their classroom.

Materials

- page 96, reproduced on an overhead transparency and for individual students
- hole punch
- binder rings

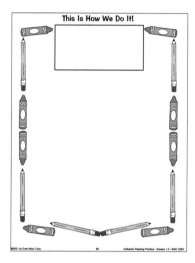

Steps to Follow

1. Using the overhead transparency, have your students dictate the steps to follow for a specific procedure. Your manual might include "how-to's" for the following:
   - opening and calendar routines
   - turning in homework
   - exiting the room for a fire drill
   - checking out a library book
   - taking attendance
   - getting permission to use the bathroom
   - visiting the nurse
   - cleaning up after an art project or center time

2. Read the directions over and revise them until you and the class are satisfied that they are complete.

3. Copy the procedure on a paper copy of the form. (Capable students might be assigned this task.)

4. Hole-punch the form. As you add procedures, compile them into a booklet using binder rings. Create a cover.

5. Display the book prominently and read the directions often.

This Is How We Do It!

Reading Directions at Learning Centers

Centers provide students with a perfect place for independent practice in reading directions.

ACTIVITIES

Hints and How-to's (Page 98)
Teacher hints and how-to's that will make centers run more smoothly.

Student Observation Checklist (Page 99)
Assess student work at learning centers with this simple checklist. Reproduce, cut, and attach to a small clipboard.

Ten Learning Centers (Pages 100–123)
Each center contains a page of teacher instructions, a student instruction sheet, and other reproducible materials as needed. The first five centers rely on pictures clues; the remaining five centers combine written directions with picture clues.

Make a Necklace Center	Build a Truck Center	Write a Riddle Center
Number Grid Center	Popcorn Problems Center	A Flying Machine Center
Write a Postcard Center	Bird in a Cage Center	
Sink or Float Center	Stones in a Bowl Center	

Following Directions Chart (Page 124)
Enlarge, laminate, and post this chart to remind students of how to follow directions at centers.

Hints and How-to's

Preparing the Centers

1. Choose the centers you wish to use. (See pages 100–123).

2. Reproduce the student center directions.

3. Make a sign of basic center directions that can be posted at each center.
   • number of people that may use the center at one time
   • how long an individual may stay at the center
   • general procedures

4. Post the basic directions and the directions for the specific center.

5. Prepare and set out the necessary materials.

Center Standards

Develop with your class a set of center standards for working in the centers. List these standards on a chart and post it in a visible place. Center standards might include:
   • proper use of the materials
   • cleanup procedures
   • appropriate behavior
   • how participants are chosen

Presenting the Centers

1. Read the "Prior Knowledge" section of the teacher direction sheet to determine if there are vocabulary words or concepts that you need to teach before introducing the center activity.

2. Gather students around the center.

3. Point out the materials to be used. Select students to demonstrate proper use of materials and equipment.

4. Read the student direction sheet and discuss each step.

5. Review center standards.

Observing Students at Centers

Use the checklist on page 99 to help you assess students' abilities to read and follow directions at a learning center.

teacher direction sheet

student direction sheet

Note: Reproduce this checklist to help assess students' skill acquisition at learning centers.

Student Observation Checklist

Student's Name: _____

Date of Observation: _____

Center Task: _____

☐ Reads task directions _____

☐ Completes assignment _____

☐ Can explain task to others _____

☐ Shares materials with others _____

☐ Displays appropriate behavior _____

☐ Follows cleanup procedures _____

Student Observation Checklist

Student's Name: _____

Date of Observation: _____

Center Task: _____

☐ Reads task directions _____

☐ Completes assignment _____

☐ Can explain task to others _____

☐ Shares materials with others _____

☐ Displays appropriate behavior _____

☐ Follows cleanup procedures _____

Make a Necklace Center

Materials
- colored macaroni (see instructions for coloring macaroni below)
- 1″ (2.5 cm) squares of construction paper with holes punched in the center (six per student)
- plastic needles or 2″ (5 cm) lengths of pipe cleaner
- yarn cut in 12″ (30.5 cm) lengths
- copy of page 101, reproduced and laminated to use as center directions
- pattern record sheet (below), reproduced for each student

Teacher Preparation
1. Color the macaroni.

   Pour the package of macaroni to be colored in a large bowl. Combine 2 tablespoons of rubbing alcohol with food coloring. The amount of food coloring you add will determine the intensity of the color. Pour the color mixture over the macaroni and stir until all the macaroni is colored. Cover a cookie sheet with paper toweling and spread colored macaroni on it to dry. Drying will take 15 to 30 minutes.

2. Thread the needles with yarn and tie to secure the yarn so that it won't pull out of the needle.

Prior Knowledge
1. Students must be able to manipulate a needle or pipe cleaner through the center of the macaroni.

2. Students must understand how to create a pattern using different colors.

3. Students must be able to follow picture directions to complete a task.

- -

Pattern Record Sheet

Name _____

This is the pattern I will use to make my necklace.

Make a Necklace

Read how to do it carefully. Follow steps: 1, 2, and 3. . . .

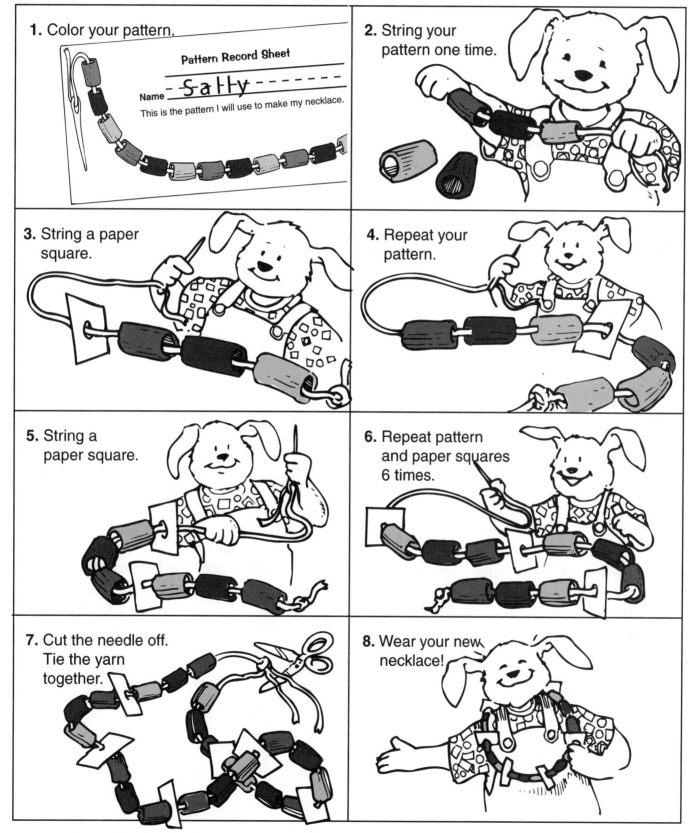

1. Color your pattern.

Pattern Record Sheet

Name —Sally——————

This is the pattern I will use to make my necklace.

2. String your pattern one time.

3. String a paper square.

4. Repeat your pattern.

5. String a paper square.

6. Repeat pattern and paper squares 6 times.

7. Cut the needle off. Tie the yarn together.

8. Wear your new necklace!

Number Grid Center

Materials
- small beans to be used for counters
- copy of the directions at the bottom of this page, enlarged and laminated to use as center directions
- page 103, reproduced for each student
- glue
- black crayon or pencil

Teacher Preparation
- Provide margarine tubs with lids (or other small containers) for the bean counters.
- Provide a spot for the grids to dry.

Prior Knowledge
1. Students must be familiar with the number words and numerals from one to ten.

2. Students must be able to write the numerals.

- -

Number Grid Center

Read how to do it carefully.
Follow steps: 1, 2, and 3. . . .

I can show what a numeral means.

1. Write your name on the number grid.	**2.** Write the numeral for each number word.	**3.** Show how many. Glue the beans down.

Grid 1 — Your Name: Pete

Number Word	Numeral	Counters
one		
two		
three		
four		
five		
six		
seven		
eight		
nine		
ten		

Grid 2 — Your Name: Pete

Number Word	Numeral	Counters
one	1	
two	2	
three		
four		
five		
six		
seven		
eight		
nine		
ten		

Grid 3 — Your Name: Pete

Number Word	Numeral	Counters
one	1	⬭
two	2	⬭ ⬭
three		
four		
five		
six		
seven		
eight		
nine		
ten		

Authentic Reading Practice, Grades 1–3 • EMC 3300

1 2 3 4 5 6 7 8 9 10

Number Grid Center

Name:

Number Word	Numeral	Counters
one		
two		
three		
four		
five		
six		
seven		
eight		
nine		
ten		

Write a Postcard Center

Materials
- pieces of lightweight cardboard or posterboard cut in 4 1/4″ x 6″ (10.8 x 15 cm) rectangles
- page 105, reproduced and laminated to use as center directions
- crayons or markers
- pencils
- address labels with student addresses prewritten
- stamps

Teacher Preparation
1. It is very difficult for young students to write their addresses in the small space provided on a postcard. Solve this problem by printing your students' addresses on adhesive labels using your classroom computer, or prewrite them by hand on labels. Students can then locate their label and stick it on the proper spot on the postcard.

2. You may choose to purchase stamped postcards from the post office to use instead of the posterboard rectangles.

3. Provide students with authentic reasons for writing a postcard. For example:
   - to announce a special event
   - to celebrate a special day
   - to thank someone for helping
   - to mark an achievement
   - to say "hello"
   - to ask for help
   - to share a poem
   - to set up a meeting

Prior Knowledge
1. Students must know their own address.

2. Students must be able to write a simple message.

3. Students must understand where the stamp should be placed on a postcard.

Name:

Write a Postcard

Read how to do it carefully. Follow steps: 1, 2, and 3. . . .

1. Put on the address label.

My Family
1234 Home
Town, State
00001

2. Put on the stamp.

My Family
1234 Home
Town, State
00001

3. Turn the postcard over and write.

Dear Family,
Can you guess who
this card is from?

You might say:

Thank you for all the things you do for me.

I am learning to read directions.

Isn't it fun to get mail?

4. Color a picture.

Dear Family,
Can you guess who
this card is from?

5. Sign the card.

Dear Family,
Can you guess who
this card is from?
Love,
Me

6. Mail the card.

MAIL

Authentic Reading Practice, Grades 1–3 • EMC 3300

Sink or Float Center

Materials
- page 107, reproduced and laminated to use as center directions
- record sheet below, reproduced for each student
- pencils and crayons
- tub of water
- cork
- pencil
- paper clip
- marble
- plastic spoon
- bar of soap
- twig

Teacher Preparation
- Collect all materials needed for the test.
- Provide a towel under the tub to soak up minor spills.
  Another towel can be used to dry the items after the test is completed.

Prior Knowledge
1. Students must understand the concepts "sink" and "float."
2. Students must understand how to fill in a record sheet.
3. Students must understand how to clean up after an activity involving water.

Name:		

Sink or Float Center

Will It Sink or Float?	sink	float
cork		
pencil		
paper clip		
marble		
plastic spoon		
soap		
twig		

Sink or Float

Read how to do it carefully.
Follow steps: 1, 2, and 3. . . .

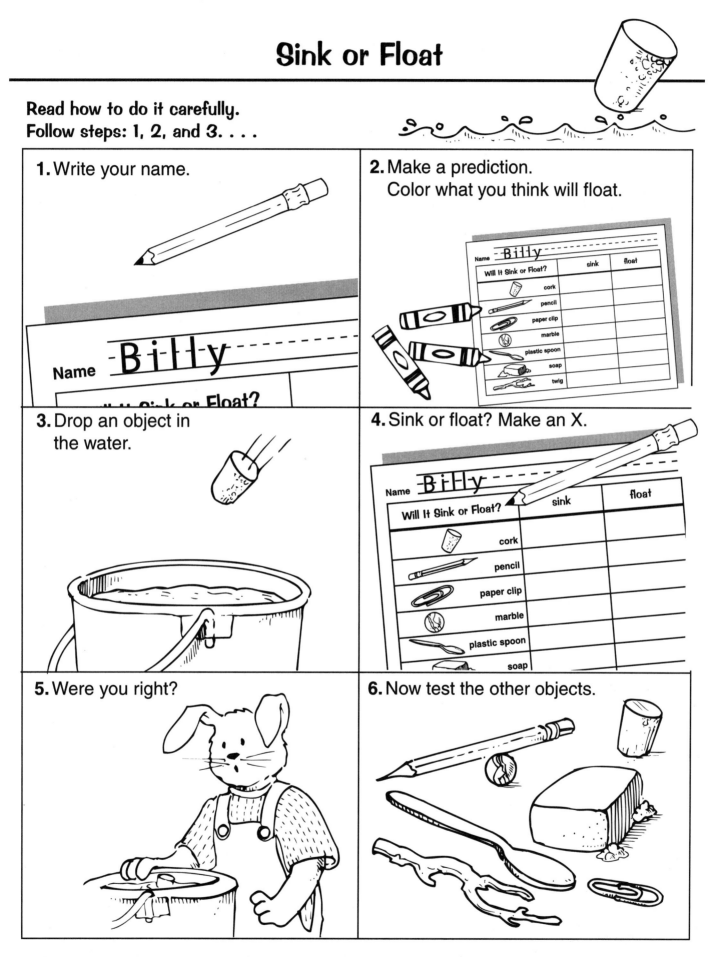

1. Write your name.

Name Billy

2. Make a prediction.
   Color what you think will float.

Name Billy		
Will It Sink or Float?	**sink**	**float**
cork		
pencil		
paper clip		
marble		
plastic spoon		
soap		
twig		

3. Drop an object in the water.

4. Sink or float? Make an X.

Name Billy		
Will It Sink or Float?	**sink**	**float**
cork		
pencil		
paper clip		
marble		
plastic spoon		
soap		

5. Were you right?

6. Now test the other objects.

Build a Truck Center

Materials
- page 109, reproduced and laminated to use as center directions
- a set of truck pieces on page 110, reproduced for each player
- rolling cube (see directions below)

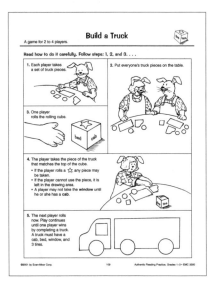

Teacher Preparation
1. Reproduce the truck pieces on construction paper. Laminate the pieces and cut them out.

2. Put each complete set of truck pieces in an envelope. Each player then lays the contents of an envelope in the center of the playing surface to begin the game.

3. Use a carpet square or a folded towel as a rolling surface to cut down on noise.

4. Make the rolling cube by writing one word on each side of a wooden or tagboard cube with a thin-tipped permanent marker.

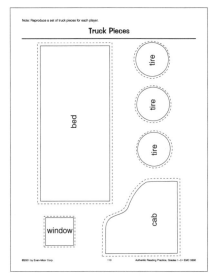

cab	bed	tire
tire	tire	window

Prior Knowledge
1. Students must be able to read the words on the rolling cube.

2. Students must recognize and be able to name the parts of a truck. They must also be able to put the truck pieces together correctly.

Build a Truck

Read how to do it carefully. Follow steps: 1, 2, and 3. . . .

1. Each player takes a set of truck pieces.

2. Put everyone's truck pieces on the table.

3. One player rolls the rolling cube.

bed **cab**

4. The player takes the piece of the truck that matches the top of the cube.

- If the player rolls a ☆, any piece may be taken.
- If the player cannot use the piece, it is left in the drawing area.
- A player may not take the **window** until he or she has a **cab**.

5. The next player rolls now. Play continues until one player wins by completing a truck. A truck must have a cab, bed, window, and 3 tires.

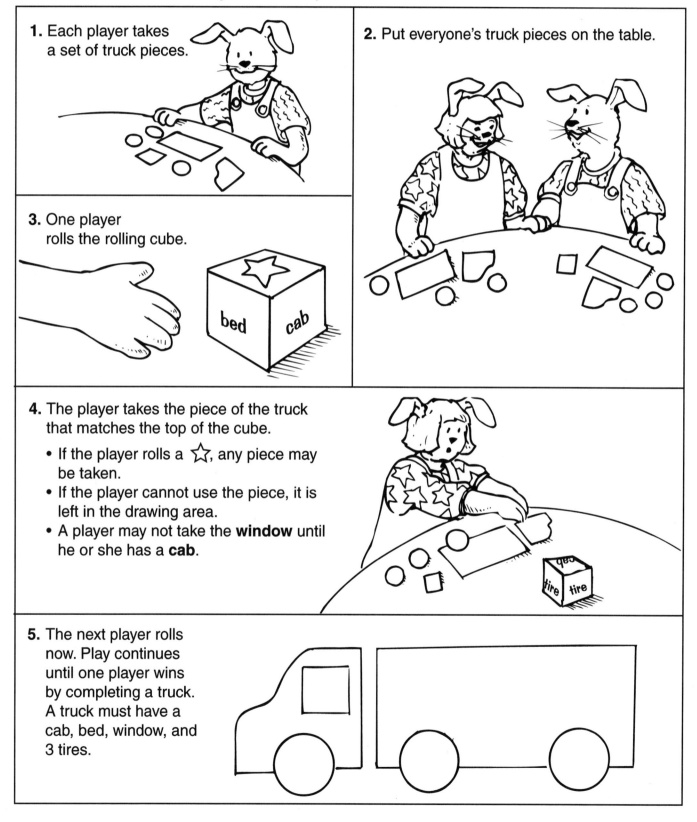

Authentic Reading Practice, Grades 1–3 • EMC 3300

Note: Reproduce a set of truck pieces for each player.

Truck Pieces

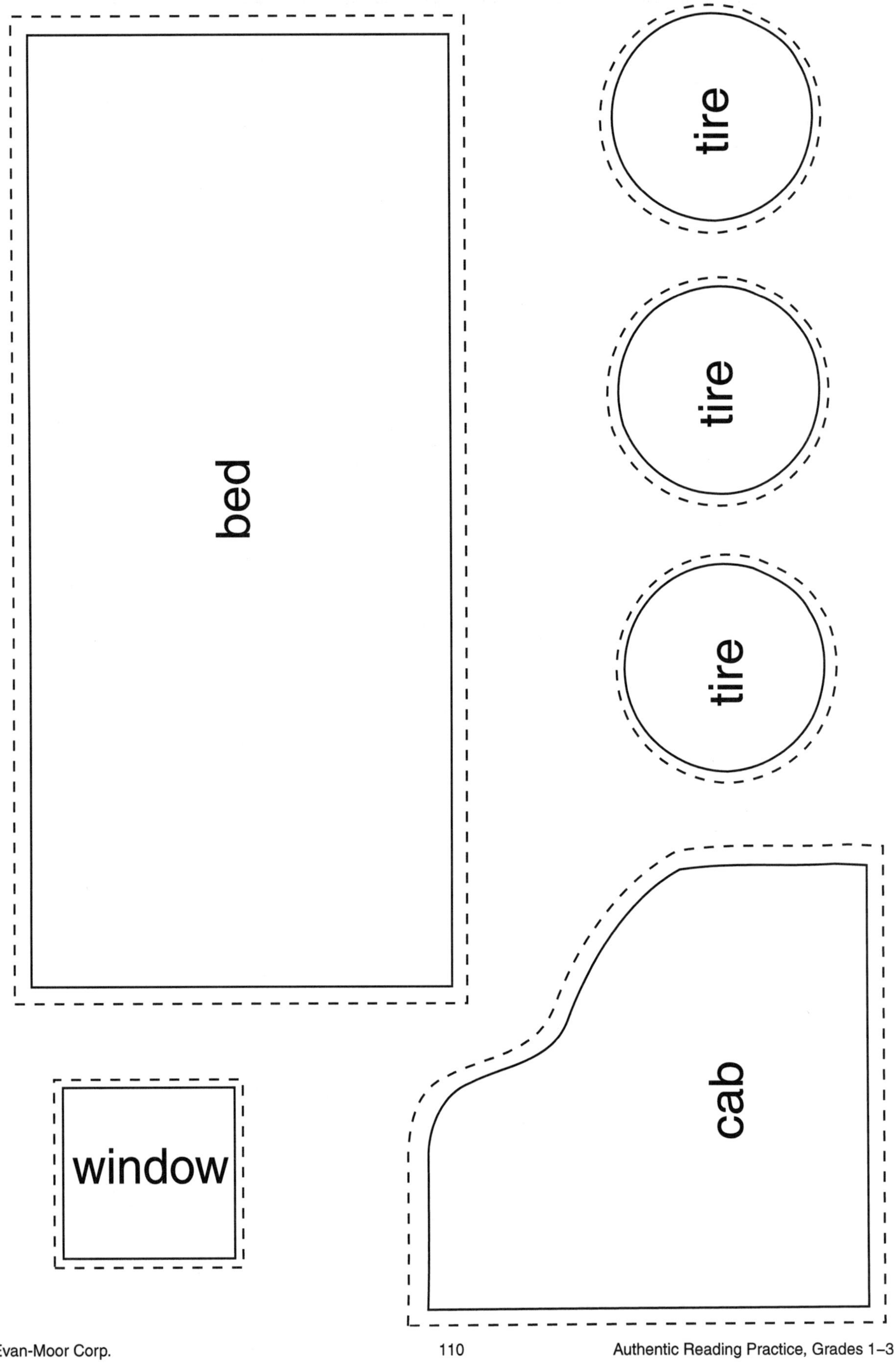

bed
tire
tire
tire
window
cab

Popcorn Problems Center

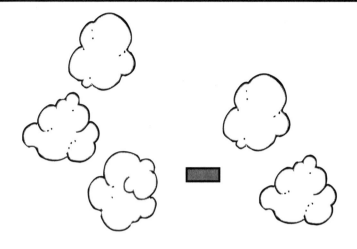

Materials
- 2 containers with lids
- unpopped and popped popcorn
- ruler
- balance scale
- instructions on page 112, reproduced for each student
- adhesive labels

Teacher Preparation
1. Put unpopped and popped popcorn (at least 10 kernels) in separate, labeled containers.

2. Place all materials at the center.

Prior Knowledge
1. Students must be able to read and understand these words:

popped	estimate	kernels
measure	unpopped	scale
row	weigh	handful

2. Students must understand how to use a ruler and a balance scale.

3. Students must have had experience with subtracting numbers and with estimation.

Popcorn Problems

Read all of the instructions. Do the steps one at a time.

1. Put 10 unpopped kernels in a row.
Measure the row.

The row of unpopped kernels is _____ long.

2. Put 10 popped kernels in a row.
Measure the row.

The row of popped kernels is _____ long.

How much longer is the row of popped kernels? _____

3. How many unpopped kernels does it take to make a row
as long as 10 popped kernels?

It takes _____ unpopped kernels.

4. Put 10 kernels of unpopped corn on one side of the scale.
Put 10 kernels of popped corn on the other side of the scale.

Which weighs the most? _____

5. Take a handful of unpopped kernels.
Estimate how many kernels are in your hand.

I think I have _____ kernels.

6. Count the handful of kernels.
How many do you have?

I have _____ kernels.

7. Do you have more or fewer kernels than your estimate?

I have _____ kernels. How many? _____
    (more - fewer)

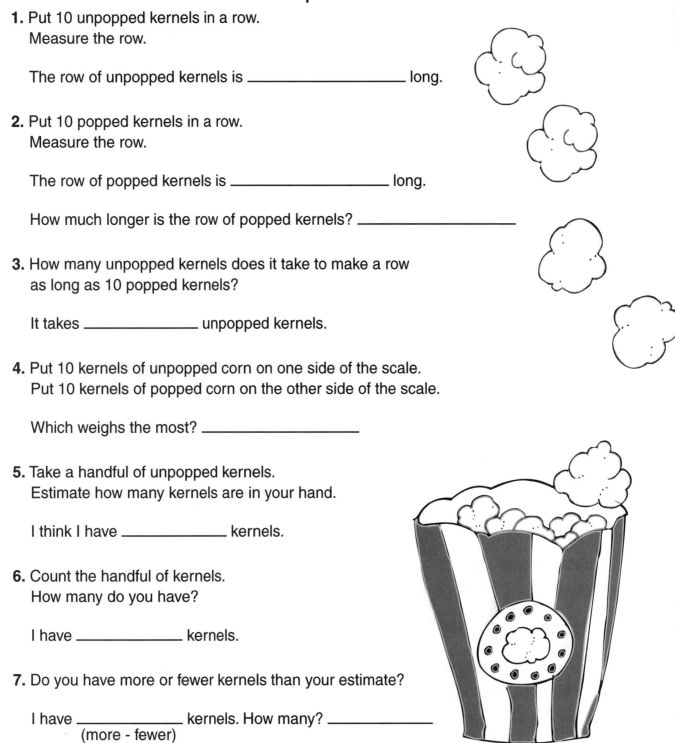

Bird in a Cage Center

Materials
- 4″ (10 cm) square of cardboard to use as a template
- tagboard pieces larger than 4″ (10 cm) square
- scissors
- plastic straws without a bendable joint
- glue
- marking pens
- instructions on page 114, reproduced and laminated to use as center directions

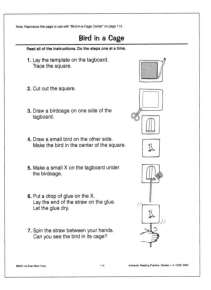

Teacher Preparation
Place all materials at the center.

Prior Knowledge
1. Students must be able to read and understand these words:

trace	square	tagboard	template
birdcage	straw	dry	between

2. Students must understand how to use a template.

3. Students must know what a birdcage looks like.

Note: Reproduce this page to use with "Bird in a Cage Center" on page 113.

Bird in a Cage

Read all of the instructions. Do the steps one at a time.

1. Lay the template on the tagboard.
Trace the square.

2. Cut out the square.

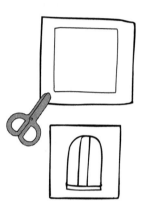

3. Draw a birdcage on one side of the
tagboard.

4. Draw a small bird on the other side.
Make the bird in the center of the square.

5. Make a small X on the tagboard under
the birdcage.

6. Put a drop of glue on the X.
Lay the end of the straw on the glue.
Let the glue dry.

7. Spin the straw between your hands.
Can you see the bird in its cage?

 Authentic Reading Practice, Grades 1–3 • EMC 3300

Stones in a Bowl Center

Materials
- 6 small, fairly flat stones
- black paint
- small wooden bowl
- 20 lima beans
- small box or other container
- instructions on page 116, reproduced and laminated to use as center directions

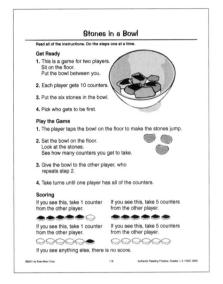

Teacher Preparation
1. Paint one side of each stone black. Leave the other side the natural color.
2. Put the lima beans in a box or container labeled "counters."
3. Place all materials at the center.

Prior Knowledge
1. Students must be able to read and understand these words:

stones	counters	facing	bowl
floor	score	point	player
bounce			

2. Students need to know how to tap the bowl on the floor to make the stones jump up and turn over.

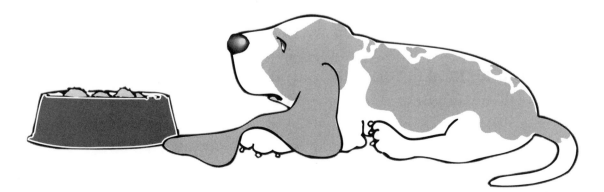

Stones in a Bowl

Read all of the instructions. Do the steps one at a time.

Get Ready

1. This is a game for two players.
   Sit on the floor.
   Put the bowl between you.

2. Each player gets 10 counters.

3. Put the six stones in the bowl.

4. Pick who gets to be first.

Play the Game

1. The player taps the bowl on the floor to make the stones jump.

2. Set the bowl on the floor.
   Look at the stones.
   See how many counters you get to take.

3. Give the bowl to the other player, who repeats step 2.

4. Take turns until one player has all of the counters.

Scoring

If you see this, take 1 counter from the other player.

If you see this, take 5 counters from the other player.

If you see this, take 1 counter from the other player.

If you see this, take 5 counters from the other player.

If you see anything else, there is no score.

Write a Riddle Center

Materials
- 9˝ x 12˝ (23 x 30.5 cm) construction paper
- pencils
- glue
- scissors
- instructions and writing form on page 118, reproduced for each student
- picture cards on pages 119 and 120, reproduced
- manila envelope

Teacher Preparation
1. Reproduce the picture cards. Glue the pages to construction paper, laminate, and cut apart.
2. Place the picture cards in an envelope.
3. Place all materials at the center.

Prior Knowledge
1. Students must be able to read and understand these words:
   riddle   clue   picture   sound   object
2. Students must understand what makes something a riddle. (Riddles give clues and ask questions.)
3. Students must know the word to describe an object (adjectives) and its actions (verbs).

Write a Riddle

1. Pick a picture.

2. Think about the object in the picture.

   What does it look like?
   What can it do?
   What sound does it make?

3. Write a riddle on the lines.

   Give clues that describe the object.

   Don't give away the object's name

4. Fold on the line.

5. Paste the picture inside.

fold

I am: _____

_____
what it looks like

I can: _____

_____
what it can do

I make this sound: _____

_____
what sound it makes

What am I?

_____

Name:

Write a Riddle

1. Pick a picture.

2. Think about the object in the picture.

   What does it look like?
   What can it do?
   What sound does it make?

3. Write a riddle on the lines.

   Give clues that describe the object.

   Don't give away the object's name.

4. Fold on the line.

5. Paste the picture inside.

fold

I am: _____

_____
what it looks like

I can: _____

_____
what it can do

I make this sound: _____

_____
what sound it makes

What am I?

_____

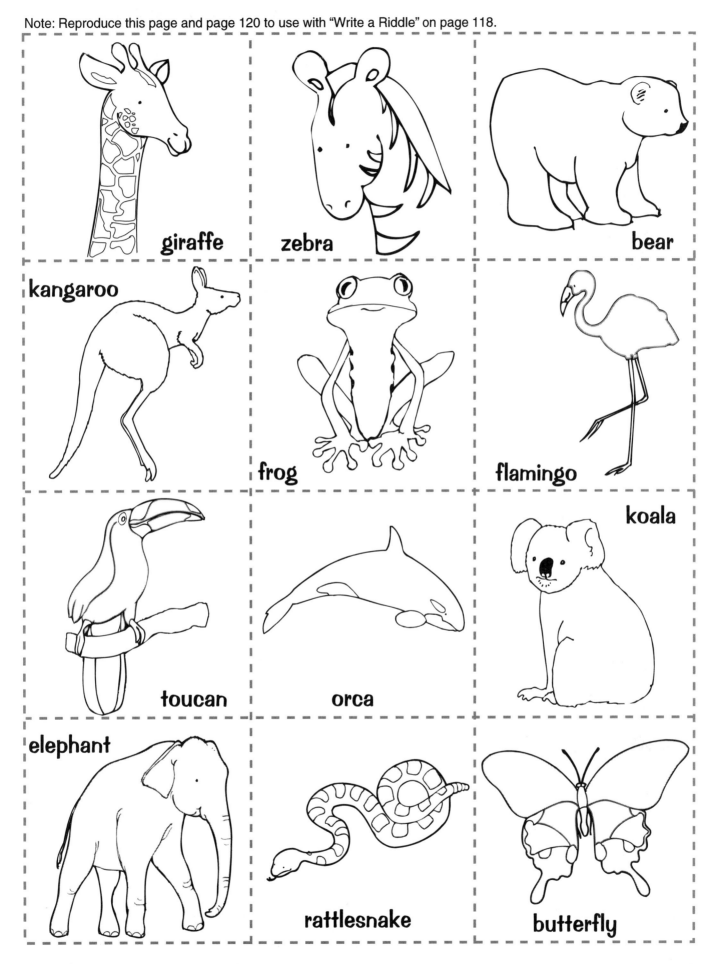

giraffe

zebra

bear

kangaroo

frog

flamingo

toucan

orca

koala

elephant

rattlesnake

butterfly

Authentic Reading Practice, Grades 1–3 • EMC 3300

helicopter	submarine	space alien
in-line skates	bicycle	hot-air balloon
ice-cream cone	pizza	rainstorm
cowboy boots	volcano	Draw your picture here.

 Authentic Reading Practice, Grades 1–3 • EMC 3300

A Flying Machine Center

Materials
- plastic straws without a bendable joint
- scissors
- tape
- measuring tape or yardstick/meterstick
- crayons or marking pens
- instructions on page 122, reproduced and laminated to use as center directions
- patterns on page 123, reproduced for each student

Teacher Preparation
Place all materials at the center.

Prior Knowledge
1. Students must be able to read and understand these words:

design	colorful	straight
strip	ring	loops
overlap	parts	permission

2. Students must know how to use a measuring instrument to measure distance.

A Flying Machine

Read all of the instructions. Do the steps one at a time.

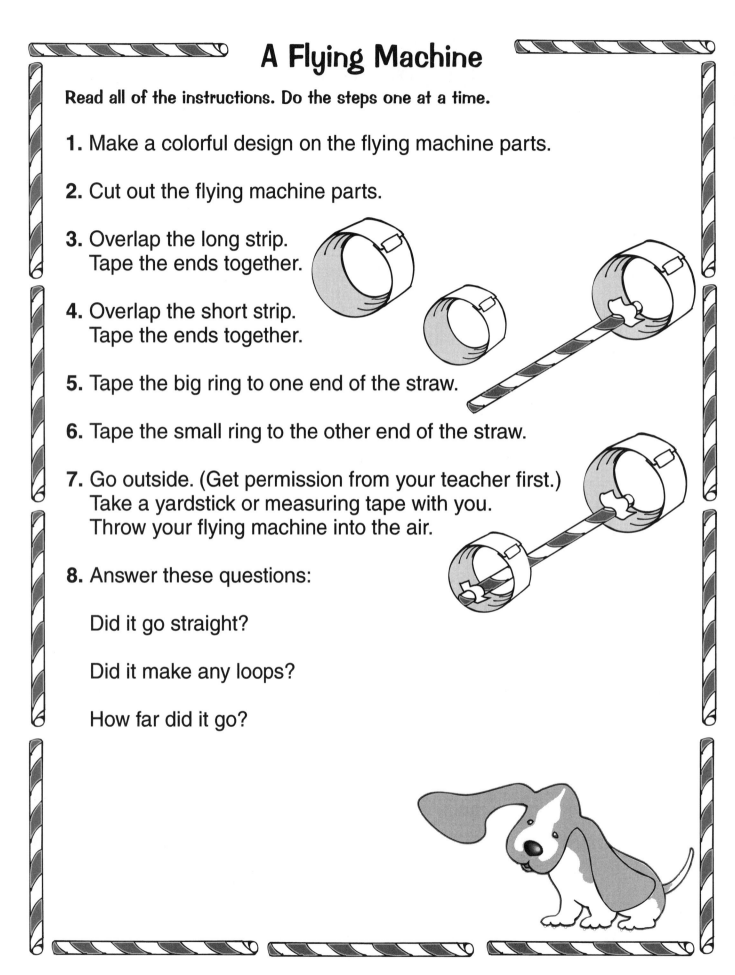

1. Make a colorful design on the flying machine parts.

2. Cut out the flying machine parts.

3. Overlap the long strip.
Tape the ends together.

4. Overlap the short strip.
Tape the ends together.

5. Tape the big ring to one end of the straw.

6. Tape the small ring to the other end of the straw.

7. Go outside. (Get permission from your teacher first.)
Take a yardstick or measuring tape with you.
Throw your flying machine into the air.

8. Answer these questions:

Did it go straight?

Did it make any loops?

How far did it go?

 Authentic Reading Practice, Grades 1–3 • EMC 3300

Note: Reproduce these patterns to use with "A Flying Machine" on page 121.

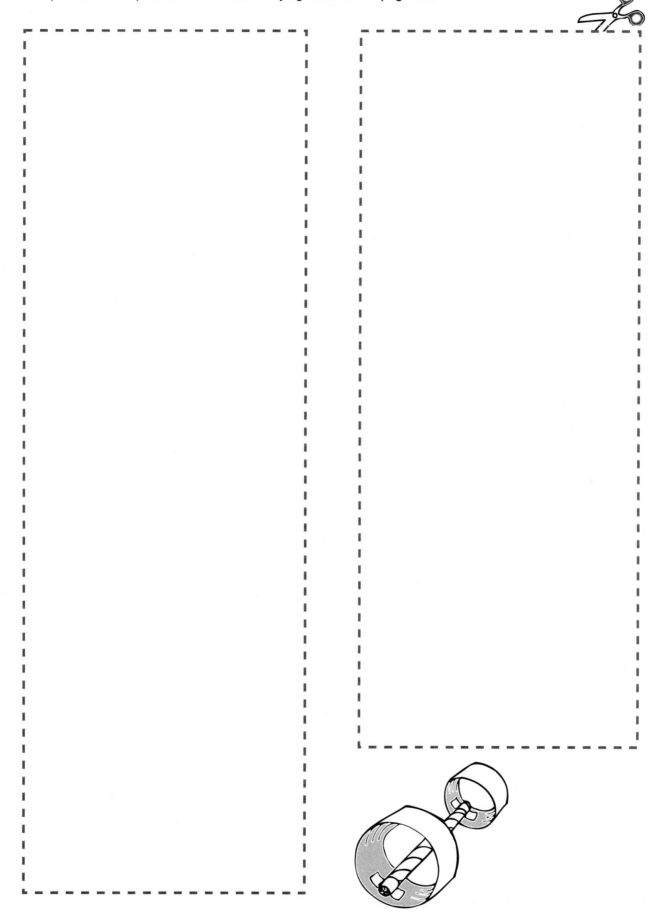

Authentic Reading Practice, Grades 1–3 • EMC 3300

Following Directions Chart

1. Read all the directions before you start.

2. Collect your materials.

3. Read each step carefully.

    a. Follow the step.

    b. Read it again to be sure you did everything.

    c. Go on to the next step.

4. Turn in your work.

5. Put things away.

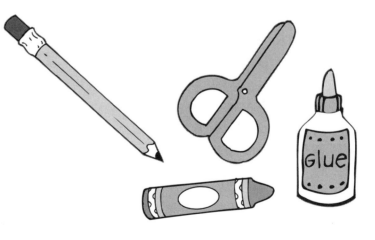

Reading to Follow Directions Skills Checklist ✓

	Students' Names									
Follows oral directions										
Reads directions to solve math problems										
Reads directions to do a science experiment										
Reads directions to do an art project										
Reads common cooking terms										
Reads and follows a simple recipe										
Understands that reading directions are part of everyday life										
Writes directions for a simple recipe										
Writes directions on how to play a game										
Reads directions at learning centers										

Part 3

Everyday Reading Skills

In this section, students will practice reading various types of material from everyday life—menus, mail, containers and tags, and maps and directories.

Reading Containers, Labels, and Price Tags

What's in that box of cereal? How do you wash that new T-shirt? What is the price of this ball cap? These questions and more can be answered by students if they know how to read containers, labels, and price tags.

ACTIVITIES

Reading Containers (Pages 128–133)
Reproduce pages 129–132 on overhead transparencies to use as visuals for the teaching ideas on page 128. Page 133 is a follow-up home practice activity.

Reading Labels (Pages 134–136)
Reproduce page 135 on an overhead transparency to use with the teaching ideas on page 134. Page 136 is a follow-up home practice activity.

Reading Price Tags (Pages 137–139)
Before using the teaching ideas on page 137, reproduce page 138 on an overhead transparency and page 139 for each pair of students.

Reading Containers

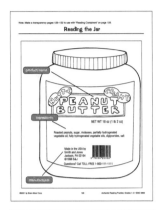

Materials
- selection of containers (boxes, jars, wrappers)
- pages 129–132, reproduced on overhead transparencies
- page 133, reproduced for individual students

Steps to Follow
1. Show the container transparencies one at a time. Ask questions such as:

    What is the name of the product?

    What is the name of the company that made/manufactured the product?

    How many servings does the package contain?

    How much does the container and product weigh?

    Can you name the first ingredient in this product?

    Where do you write or call if you have a question about the product?

    How do you prepare or cook the product?

    Are there any words telling you why you should use it?

    What does the nutritional information tell you?

2. Divide the class into small groups. Give each group a product container. Ask them to read as much of the information on the container as they can and to make a list of what they learn.

3. Share information gathered by each group. List any items that were the same on all containers.

4. Have students complete page 133 at home. Share the information gathered when the sheets are returned.

Note: Make a transparency of pages 129–132 to use with "Reading Containers" on page 128.

Reading the Jar

product name

Nutty **Creamy**

PEANUT BUTTER

NET WT 18 oz (1 lb 2 oz)

ingredients

Roasted peanuts, sugar, molasses, partially hydrogenated vegetable oil, fully hydrogenated vegetable oils, diglycerides, salt

Made in the USA by
Smith and Jones
Jackson, PA 02164
©1996 S&J

Questions? Call TOLL-FREE 1-800-111-1111

3 78083 218169

manufacturer

Reading the Lid

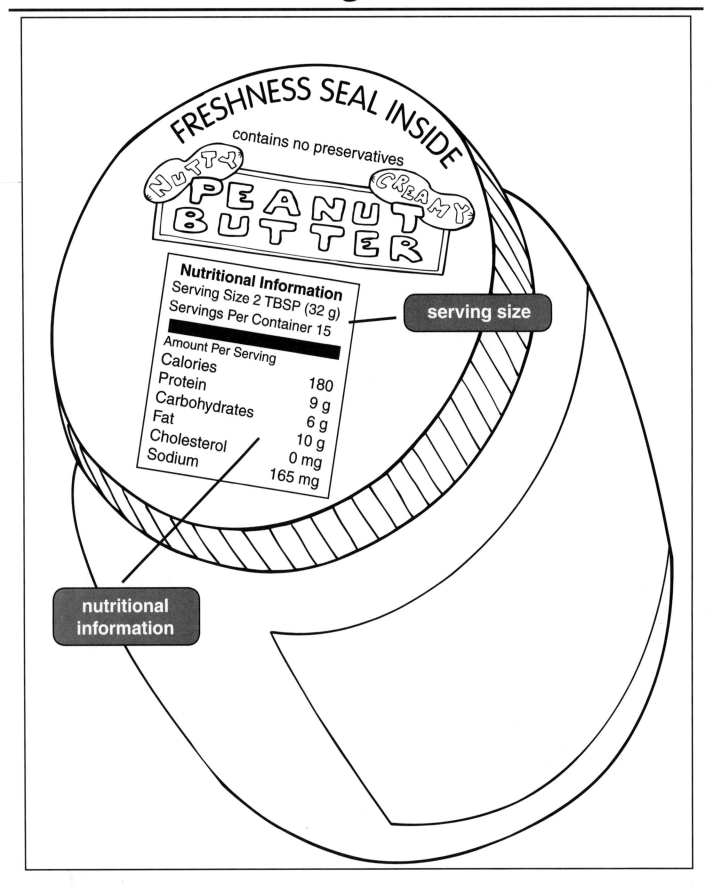

FRESHNESS SEAL INSIDE

contains no preservatives

NUTTY CREAMY

PEANUT BUTTER

Nutritional Information
Serving Size 2 TBSP (32 g)
Servings Per Container 15

Amount Per Serving
Calories
Protein   180
Carbohydrates   9 g
Fat   6 g
Cholesterol   10 g
Sodium   0 mg
                           165 mg

serving size

nutritional information

Authentic Reading Practice, Grades 1–3 • EMC 3300

Reading the Box

Favorite Foods

Try all of Favorite Foods Pudding in a Cup flavors
- vanilla
- tapioca
- banana

Favorite Foods

- *Pack in lunches*
- *Needs no refrigeration*
- *No preservatives*

PUDDING IN A CUP

Chocolate

Made with Nonfat Milk

MILK

4 - 3 ½ OZ. cups
Net WT. 14 OZ. (397 g)

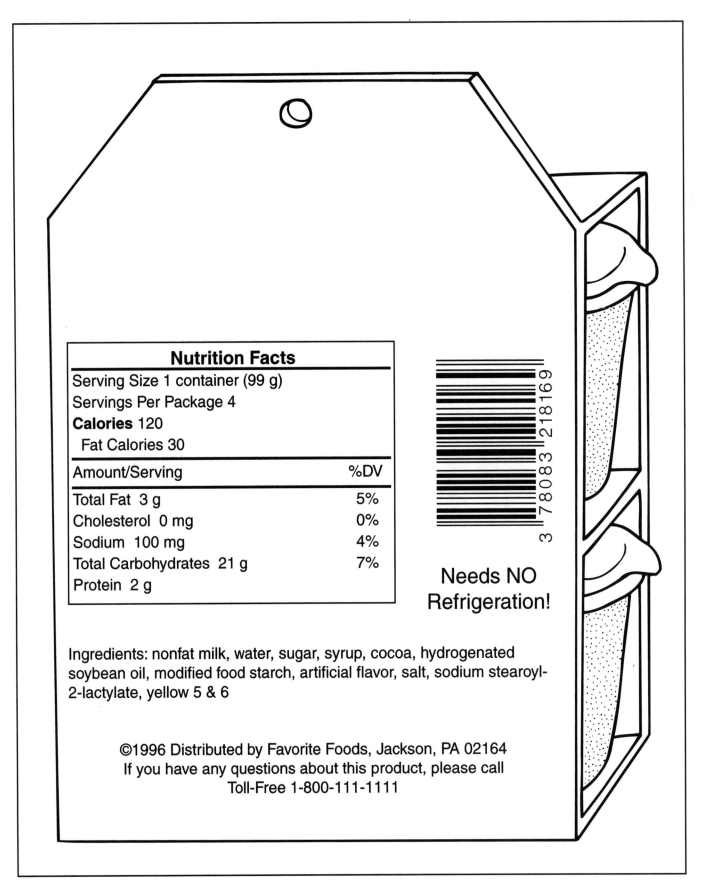

Nutrition Facts

Serving Size 1 container (99 g)

Servings Per Package 4

Calories 120

Fat Calories 30

Amount/Serving	%DV
Total Fat 3 g	5%
Cholesterol 0 mg	0%
Sodium 100 mg	4%
Total Carbohydrates 21 g	7%
Protein 2 g	

Needs NO
Refrigeration!

Ingredients: nonfat milk, water, sugar, syrup, cocoa, hydrogenated
soybean oil, modified food starch, artificial flavor, salt, sodium stearoyl-
2-lactylate, yellow 5 & 6

©1996 Distributed by Favorite Foods, Jackson, PA 02164
If you have any questions about this product, please call
Toll-Free 1-800-111-1111

Name:

Reading Containers

Pick a jar, a box, or a package in your kitchen.
Read the label. (Ask for help with words you can't figure out.)
Answer these questions.

1. What is the product's name?

_____

2. What is the name of the company that made it?

_____

3. What is the size of a serving?

_____

4. Where was it made?

_____

5. What are the first two ingredients?

_____

Draw a picture of the container here.

Reading Labels

Materials

- selection of clothing with easy-to-read labels (the lost and found is a great resource)
- page 135, reproduced on an overhead transparency
- page 136, reproduced for individual students

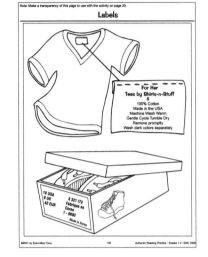

Steps to Follow

1. Hold up several pieces of clothing. Select students to find the labels.

2. Read the labels to students or ask volunteers to read them. Discuss the information on the labels and develop the meaning of any new terms.

3. Ask, "Why might you need to read the labels?" (to find the size, to find out what it is made of, to find out how to clean it, etc.)

4. Show the transparency of page 135. Read and discuss the information on the labels. Explain that some labels have information written in other languages. Ask why this might be necessary.

5. Divide students into small groups to read and share information they find on their own clothing (jackets, coats, shoes, etc.) or on clothing you provide.

6. Have students complete page 136 at home. Share the information gathered when the sheets are returned.

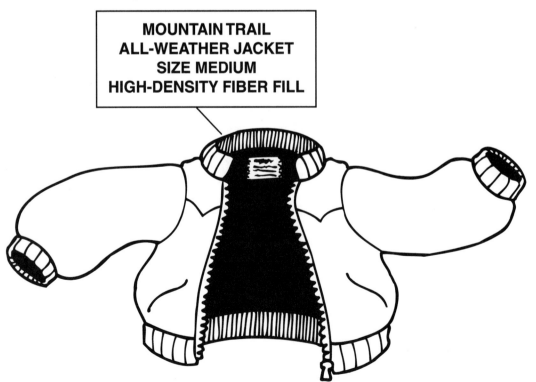

**MOUNTAIN TRAIL
ALL-WEATHER JACKET
SIZE MEDIUM
HIGH-DENSITY FIBER FILL**

Note: Make a transparency of this page to use with "Reading Labels" on page 134.

Labels

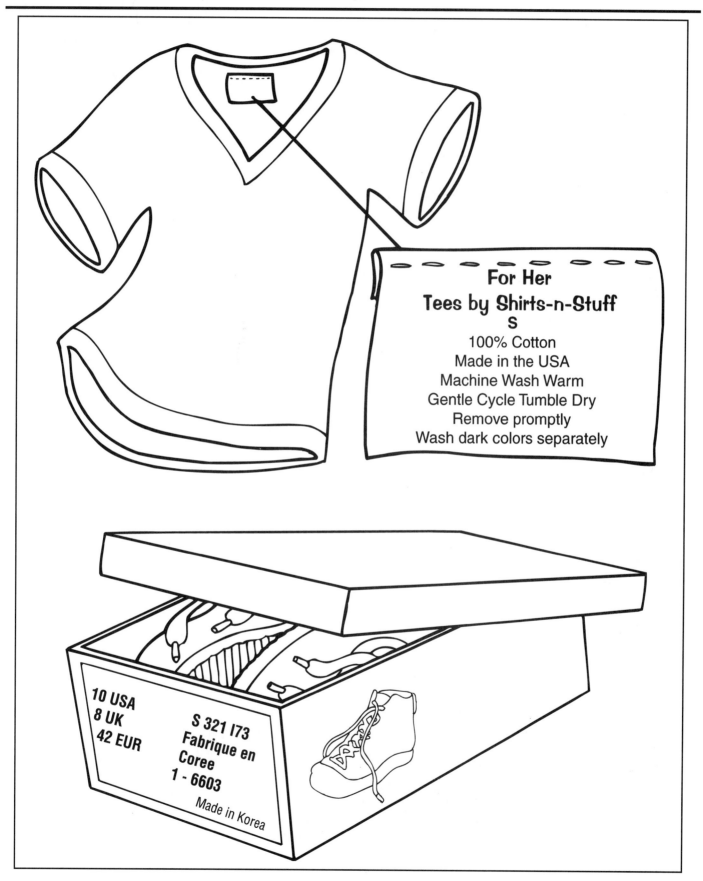

For Her
Tees by Shirts-n-Stuff
S
100% Cotton
Made in the USA
Machine Wash Warm
Gentle Cycle Tumble Dry
Remove promptly
Wash dark colors separately

10 USA
8 UK
42 EUR

S 321 I73
Fabrique en
Coree
1 - 6603

Made in Korea

Reading Labels

Read labels on clothes at home.
Pick one label and answer these questions.

1. What kind of clothing did you pick?

_____

2. What is the name of the company that made it?

_____

3. What size is it?

_____

4. Where was it made?

_____

5. How do you clean it?

_____

Draw the front of the label here.

Reading Price Tags

Materials
- selection of price tags (include those with only the cost of the item and others that provide more information)
- page 138, reproduced on an overhead transparency
- page 139, reproduced for pairs of students

Steps to Follow
1. Use the overhead transparency to introduce a simple and a more complicated price tag. Compile a list of items that might be found on a tag. Write the list on the chalkboard.

2. Pass out a selection of tags. Have students work in pairs or small groups to read the information provided on their tags. Have them refer to the list on the chalkboard to see if their tags contain the same information.

3. Have each group share what they learned. Add any new items to the list on the chalkboard.

4. Using page 139, have pairs of students design their own tag for a piece of clothing.

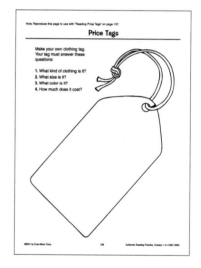

Note: Make a transparency of this page to use with "Reading Price Tags" on page 137.

Price Tags

$26.95

Sandals
Size 6
$18.95

Tees by Shirts-n-Stuff

3344	00115	4346	691
Class	**Vendor**	**Style**	**Color**

Light Pink SMALL

Comparable Price $14.00

OUR PRICE $8.99

Note: Reproduce this page to use with "Reading Price Tags" on page 137.

Price Tags

Make your own clothing tag.
Your tag must answer these
questions:

1. What kind of clothing is it?
2. What size is it?
3. What color is it?
4. How much does it cost?

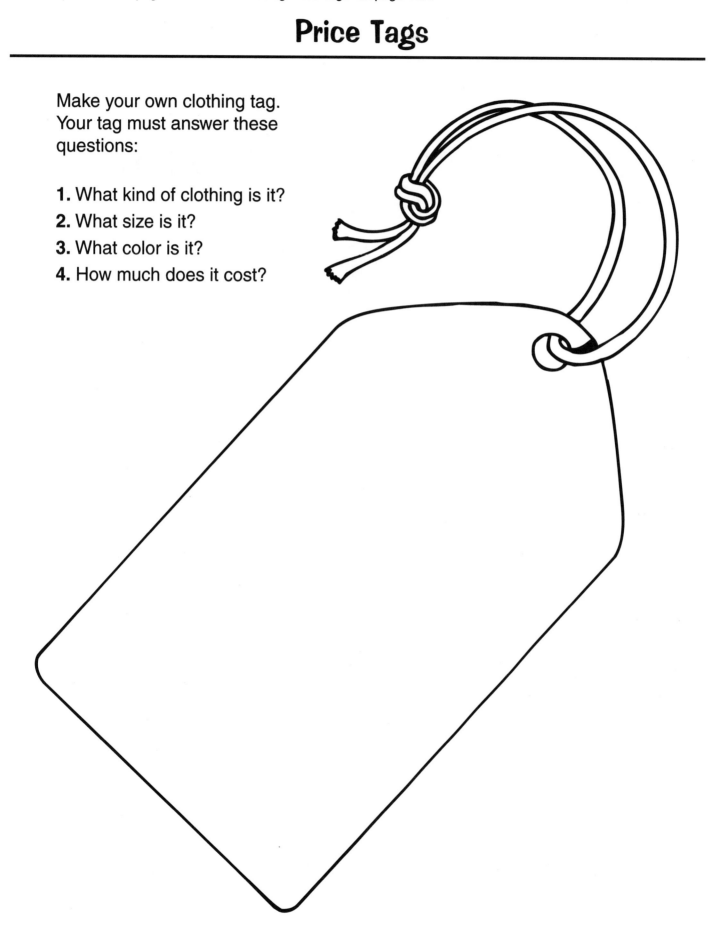

Reading Maps & Directories

There'll be no directionally challenged students in your classroom when you systematically teach how to read simple maps and directories.

ACTIVITIES

Words for Finding Your Way Around (Page 141)
The teaching ideas provided will get your students started reading words used in finding one's way around.

Getting Around at School (Page 142)
Introduce a "You are here" type of map with a simple diagram of your school.

At the Mall (Pages 143–146)
Reading store directories and mall maps are practiced on these pages.

Beginning Map Practice (Pages 147–151)
Complete these reproducibles as a class or have students work in pairs and check work as a class.

Words for Finding Your Way Around

Materials
- sentence strips and/or word cards
- marking pen

Steps to Follow

1. Write the following words and phrases on sentence strips.

left	enter
walk	north
east	right
exit	south
west	turn left
keep out	detour
emergency exit	around the corner
under the overpass	school crossing
down the road	through the tunnel
over the river	up the mountain

don't walk

next right

on the bridge

do not enter

wet paint

2. Show each card. Read it with your students. Discuss what the word or phrase means. Have students read aloud as you go through the cards again.

3. Display several of the cards. Give information about one of the cards. Ask students to read the card you are describing.

This word says you can go in through the door. (enter)

This word tells you not to go yet. (stop)

This phrase tells to be careful because children might be in the road. (school crossing)

4. Place the word cards in a place where students can practice reading them independently.

Getting Around at School

Large department stores, shopping malls, amusement parks, zoos, etc., often have maps or charts to help people find their way around. A large **X** and the words "You are here" tell you where to begin.

Materials
• white butcher paper
• yardstick or meterstick
• black marking pen
• diagram of your school (see your fire drill materials)

Steps to Follow

1. Draw a simple diagram of your school on a large sheet of butcher paper. Label the various rooms and outside areas. Make a large **X** and write the words *You are here* on your classroom.

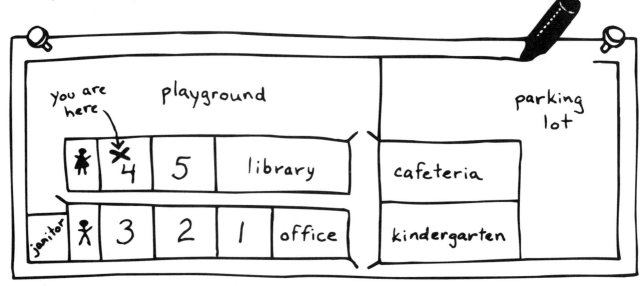

2. Have students use the map to locate places you name. Ask questions such as:

How do you get from here to the cafeteria?

What is the quickest way to the playground from here?

Where would you go if we needed a mop to clean up a mess?

How many classrooms do we have in our school?

Which way should the principal come if we needed him or her in a hurry?

At the Mall

Materials
- page 144 and 146, reproduced on overhead transparencies
- page 145, reproduced for pairs of students or for individuals

Steps to Follow

1. Show the transparency of the mall map on page 144. Have students read the map to answer questions about the locations of shops, restaurants, and bathrooms. Ask questions such as:

   How do you know where to start reading the map?

   How many stores are in this mall?

   Where would you go to buy something to eat?

   Can you buy a new bicycle at the mall?

   What shops are between the video store and the department store?

2. Have students complete page 145 for independent practice individually or in pairs.

3. Show the transparency of the department store directory on page 146. Ask questions such as:

   What does this chart tell you?

   On which floor would you find a jacket for your dad?

   What is sold on the 4th floor?

4. Take a field trip to a large department store in your community. Divide the class into groups, giving each group a department to locate and a series of tasks to do at that location. For example, you might send one group and their chaperone to the sporting goods department to find out about the different types of bicycles sold there. Another group might have to locate the linens department to find out how many different sizes of sheets are available.

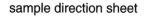
sample direction sheet

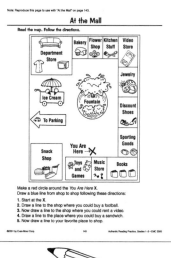
sample student sheet

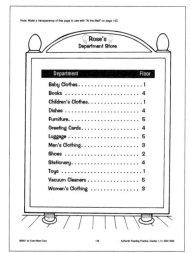

Note: Make a transparency of this page to use with "At the Mall" on page 143.

At the Mall

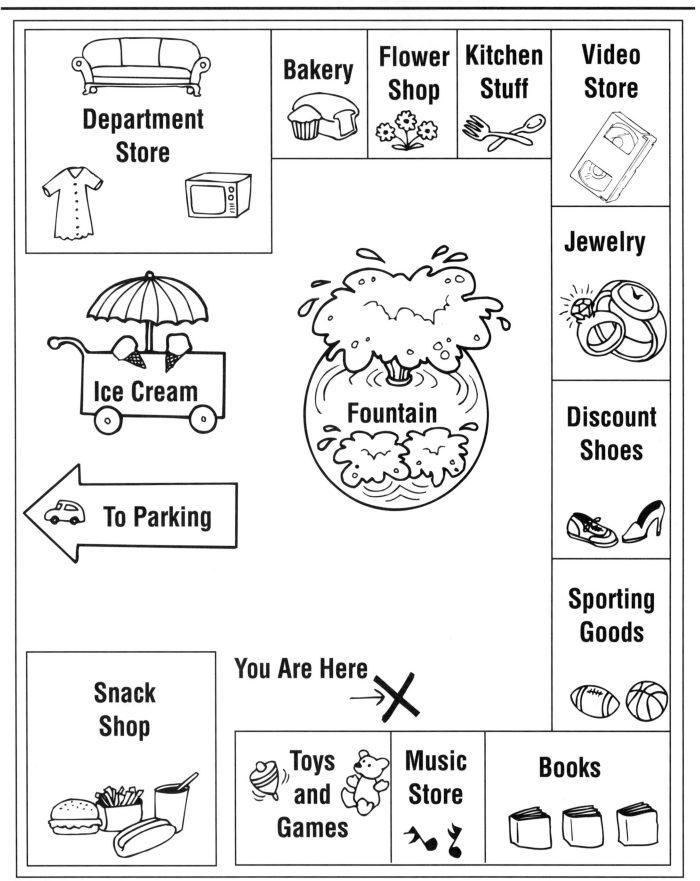

Note: Reproduce this page to use with "At the Mall" on page 143.

At the Mall

Read the map. Follow the directions.

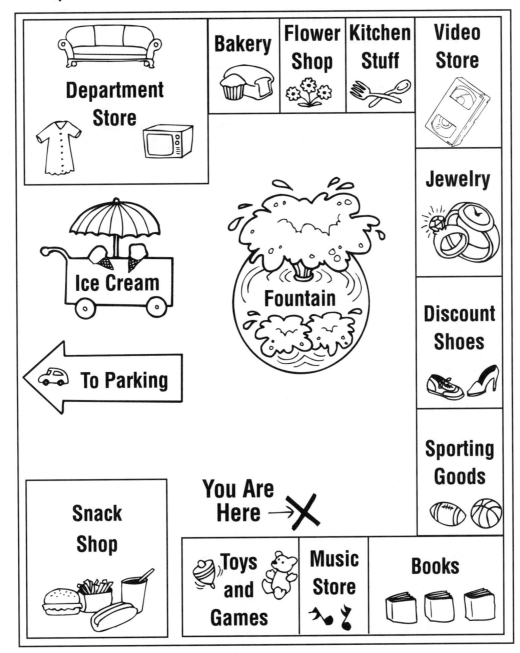

Make a red circle around the *You Are Here* **X**.

Draw a blue line from shop to shop following these directions:

1. Start at the **X**.

2. Draw a line to the shop where you could buy a football.

3. Now draw a line to the shop where you could rent a video.

4. Draw a line to the place where you could buy a sandwich.

5. Now draw a line to your favorite place to shop.

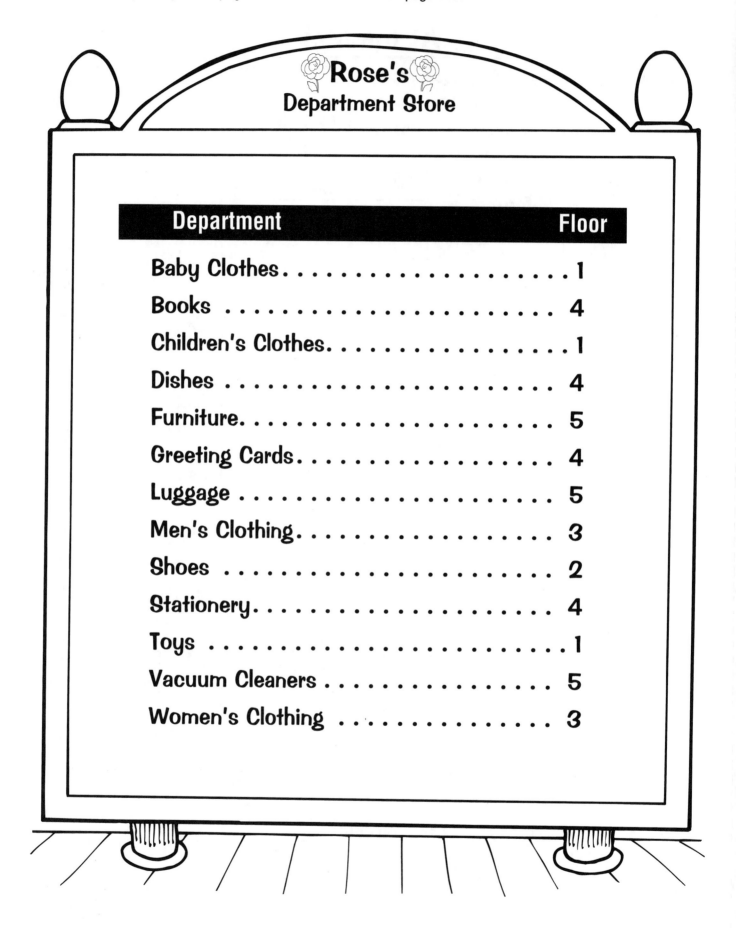

Rose's Department Store

Department	Floor
Baby Clothes	1
Books	4
Children's Clothes	1
Dishes	4
Furniture	5
Greeting Cards	4
Luggage	5
Men's Clothing	3
Shoes	2
Stationery	4
Toys	1
Vacuum Cleaners	5
Women's Clothing	3

Name:

Escape from the Maze

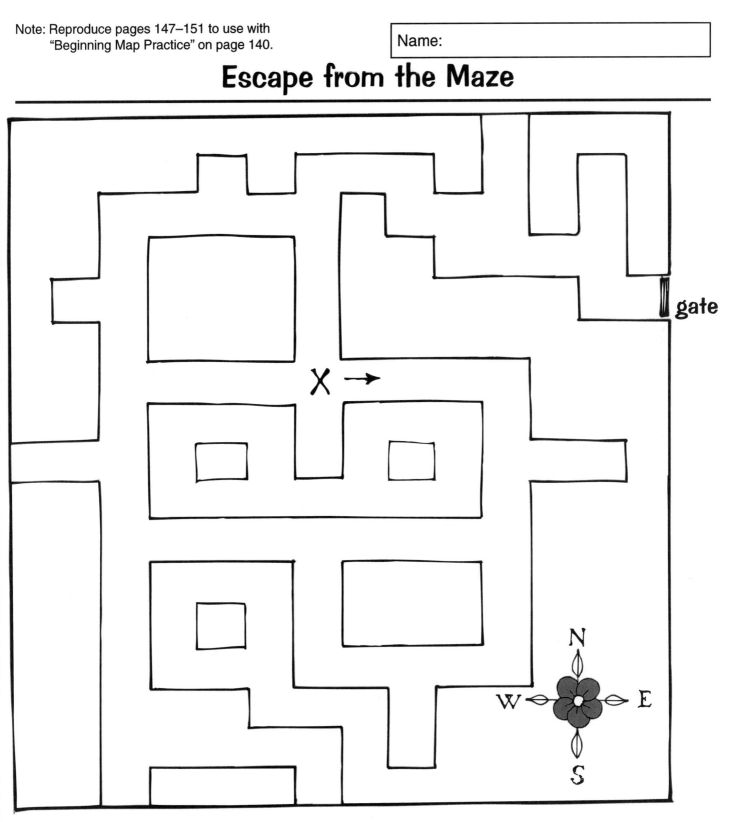

gate

Follow these instructions to get out of the maze.

1. Start at the **X**.
2. Go east to the wall.
3. Now go south as far as you can.
4. Go west.
5. Go north.
6. Now go west again.
7. Go north as far as you can, and then turn east.
8. Can you find your way to the gate now?

To Johnny's House

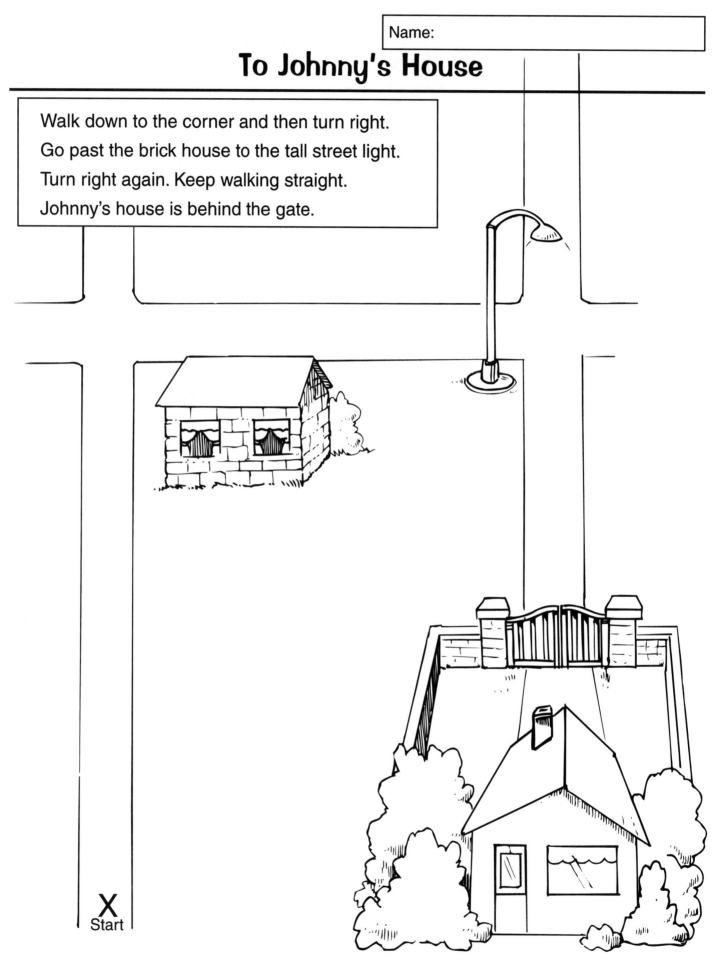

Walk down to the corner and then turn right.

Go past the brick house to the tall street light.

Turn right again. Keep walking straight.

Johnny's house is behind the gate.

X
Start

Name:

Home to the Castle

Can you help the knight and princess get home?
You must go from the ship to the castle.
Read the instructions.
Draw a line to show the path home.

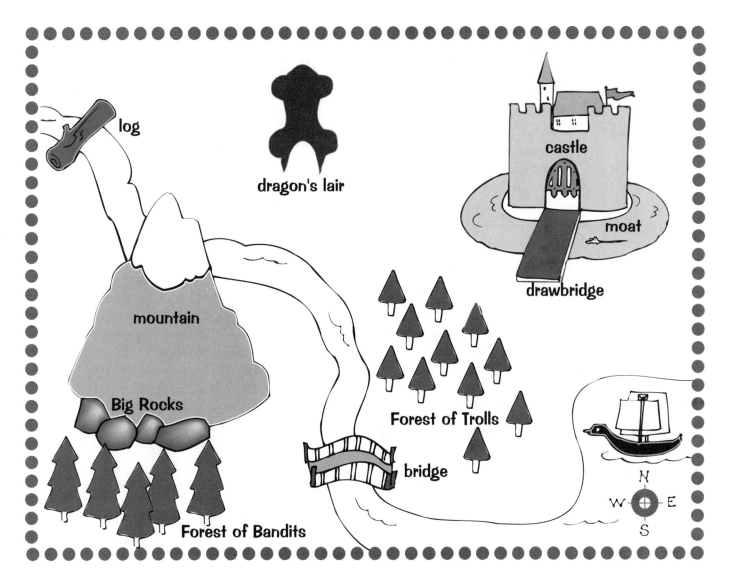

1. Start at the ship.
2. Go west to the bridge.
3. Go over the bridge.
4. Keep going west to the Big Rocks.
5. Go north past the mountain.

6. Walk across the log. Don't fall in.
7. Turn east and tiptoe past the dragon's lair.
8. Keep going east to the castle moat.
9. Walk along the moat to the drawbridge.
10. Walk over the drawbridge into the castle.

Welcome home!

Around the Amusement Park

Use this map to help you answer the questions.

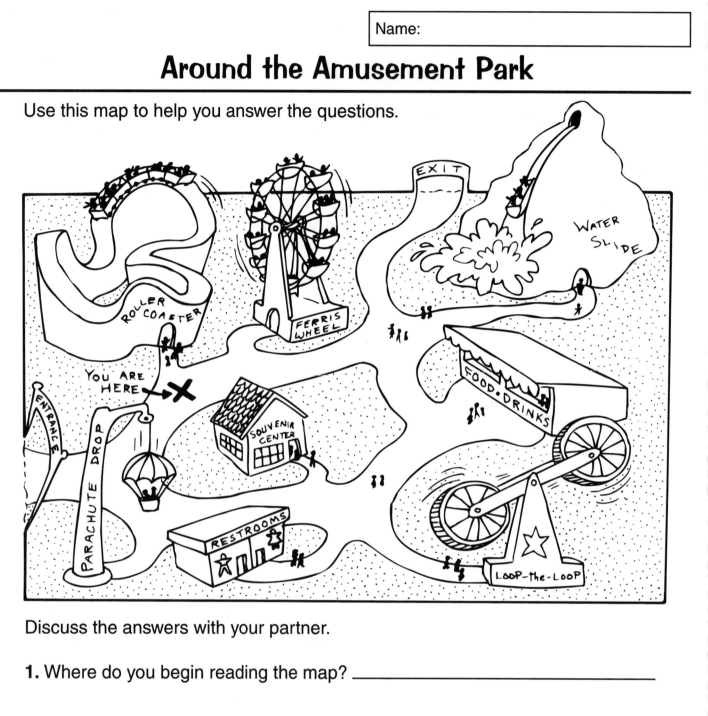

Discuss the answers with your partner.

1. Where do you begin reading the map? _____

2. What is between the Roller Coaster and the Water Slide? _____

3. Draw the quickest way from the Water Slide to the restrooms. _____

4. Is there anywhere to buy food? _____

5. What do you walk by going from the Loop-the-Loop to the Parachute Drop?

In the United States

This map shows the United States of America.
It is divided into 50 states.
You will need to look at a real map of the United States to help you do this page.

1. Write your initials on the state where you live.
2. Color California red.
3. Make a green circle around Florida.
4. Make an orange **X** on Hawaii.

5. Color Alaska blue.
6. Make a brown **X** on Texas.
7. Write **CO** on Colorado.
8. Color Lake Michigan blue.

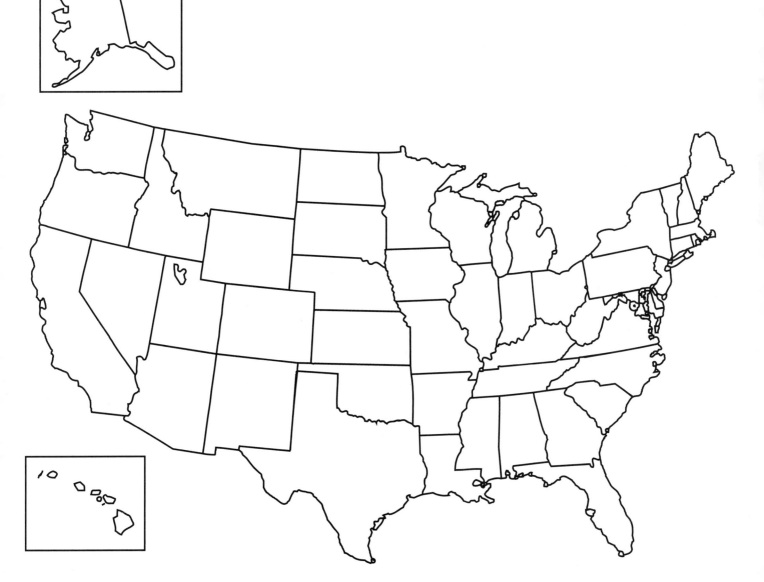

Reading the Mail

Brainstorm with your class and list all the things that arrive by mail. Bring samples to class to share—letters, postcards, greeting cards, catalogs, junk mail, invitations, magazines, etc.

ACTIVITIES

Letters and Postcards (pages 153–156)
Reproduce pages 154–156 to use with the teaching ideas on page 153.

Invitations (pages 157–159)
Have students recall invitations they have received or sent. Ask, "What does an invitation tell you?" Show some sample invitations to verify the common element of invitations. Reproduce pages 157–159 for students to write an invitation to an imaginary party. Whenever possible, have students write real invitations.

Real Writing Activities (Pages 160–162)
Reproduce pages 160–162 to use when providing opportunities for students to write letters to each other and to people outside of school. Provide legitimate reasons to write, such as:
  • to students in another class
  • to a family member or friend
  • to experts to ask questions on topics being studied
  • to places to ask for information
  • to a favorite author
  • to a public figure to state an opinion about a current event

A Mail Center (Page 163)
Make mail an ongoing feature of your classroom with this permanent center.

Letters and Postcards

Materials
- real letters and postcards
- pages 154, 155, and 156, reproduced on overhead transparencies
- pages 155 and 156, reproduced for individual students

Steps to Follow

1. Show the transparencies of the letter and the envelope. Discuss the parts of both.

2. Show the transparency of the postcard on page 156. With an erasable marker, fill in the card model to show what goes on each side.

3. Using pages 155 and 156, let students practice addressing an envelope and writing a postcard.

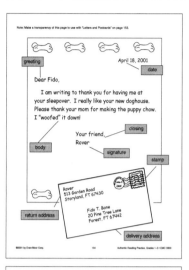

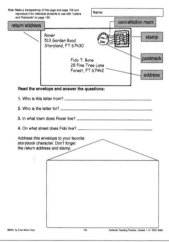

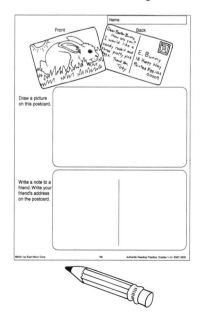

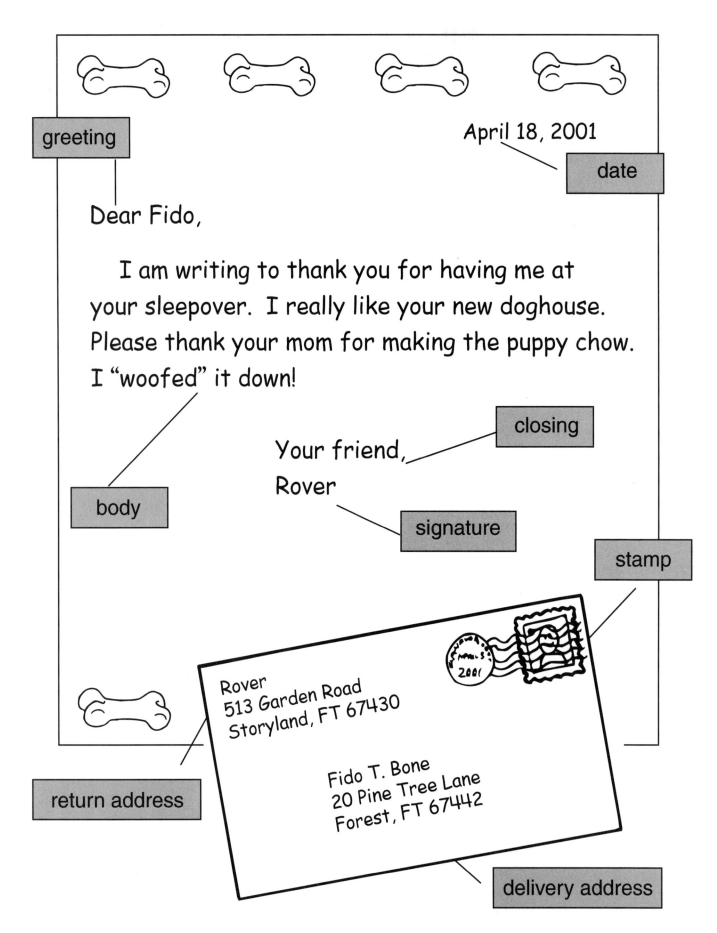

greeting

April 18, 2001

date

Dear Fido,

I am writing to thank you for having me at your sleepover. I really like your new doghouse. Please thank your mom for making the puppy chow. I "woofed" it down!

body

closing

Your friend,
Rover

signature

stamp

return address

Rover
513 Garden Road
Storyland, FT 67430

Fido T. Bone
20 Pine Tree Lane
Forest, FT 67442

delivery address

Note: Make a transparency of this page and page 156 and reproduce them for individual students to use with "Letters and Postcards" on page 153.

Name:

return address
cancellation mark
stamp
postmark
address
Rover
513 Garden Road
Storyland, FT 67430
Fido T. Bone
28 Pine Tree Lane
Forest, FT 67442
2001

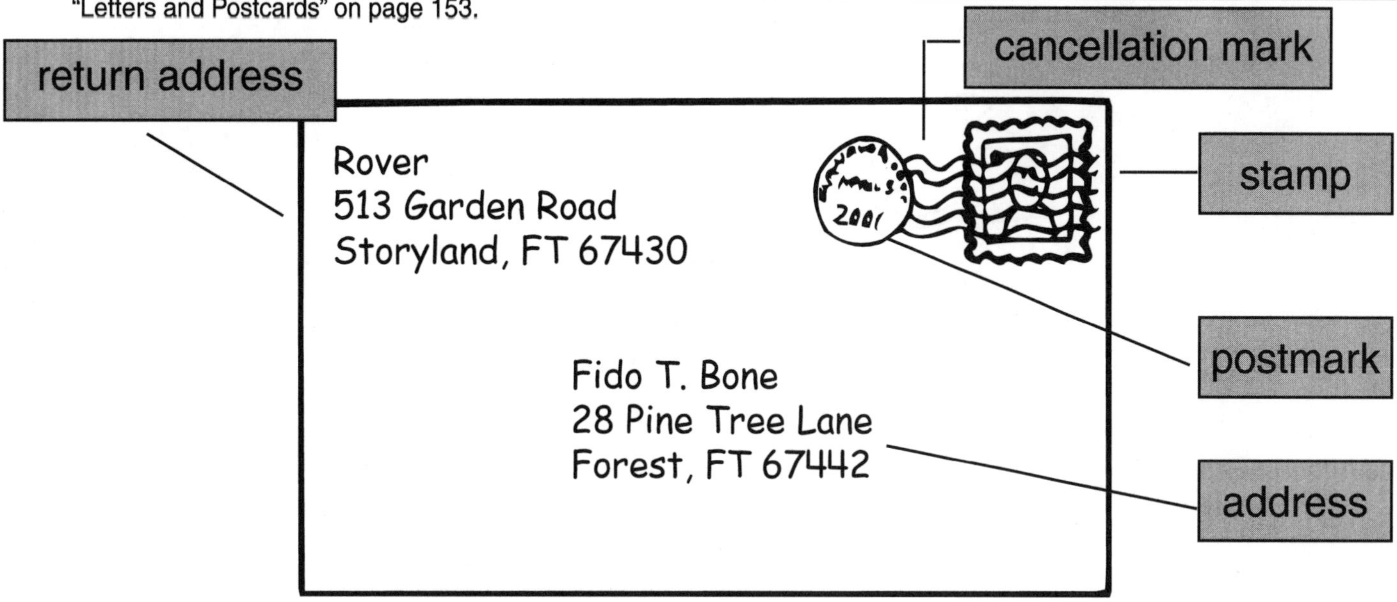

Read the envelope and answer the questions:

1. Who is this letter from? ______________________________

2. Who is the letter for? ______________________________

3. In what town does Rover live? ______________________________

4. On what street does Fido live? ______________________________

Address this envelope to your favorite storybook character. Don't forget the return address and stamp.

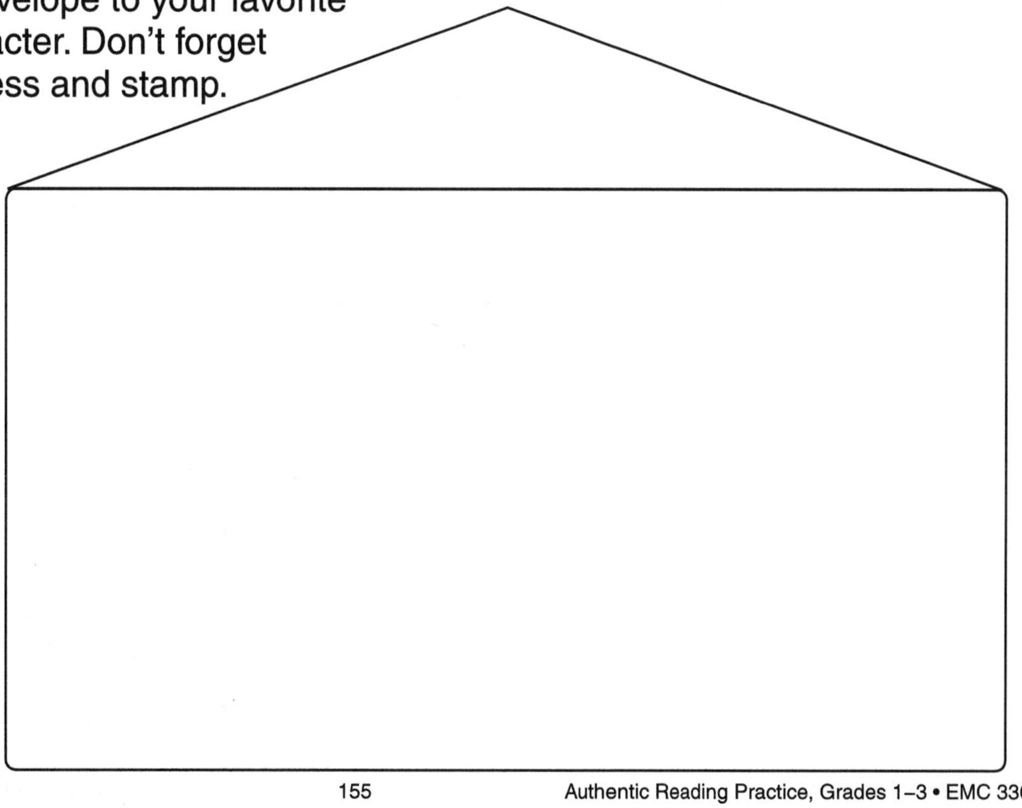

Front

Back

Dear Easter Bunny,
How are you?
I would like a
candy rabbit and
three pretty pink
eggs. Thank You,
Toby

E. Bunny
18 Hoppy Way
Painted Egg, USA
00009

Draw a picture on this postcard.

Write a note to a friend. Write your friend's address on the postcard.

Note: Reproduce pages 157–159 to use with "Invitations" on page 152.

Name:

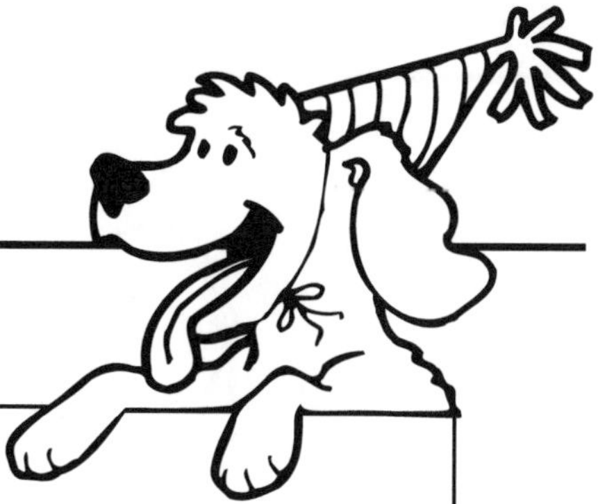

Think about a kind of party you could give.
Fill in this invitation to invite someone to your party.

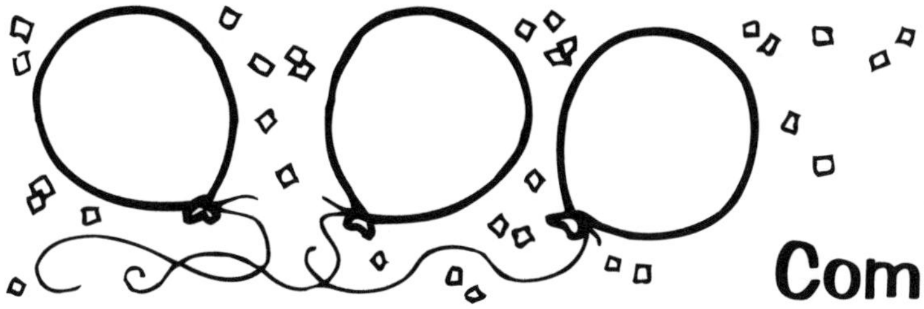

Come to My Party

Kind of Party ____________________

Place ____________________

Day ____________________

Time ____________________

RSVP to ____________________

Telephone Number ____________________

Say yes!

It's a Party!

fold

fold

Please Come

For: _____

Date: _____

Time: _____

Place: _____

1. Color.

2. Cut.

3. Fold.

4. Write.

It is going to be a party!

For: _____
Date: _____
Time: _____
Place: _____

Hooray!

We will have fun.

Can you come?

fold

fold

Draw the present under the flap.

        Authentic Reading Practice, Grades 1–3 • EMC 3300

Note: Reproduce pages 160–162 to use with "Real Writing Activities" on page 152.

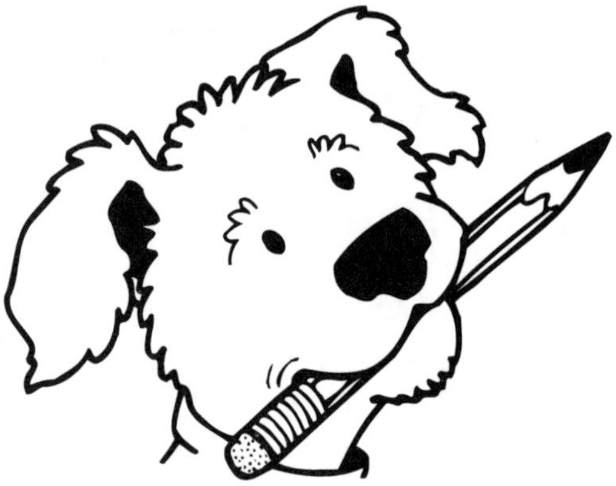

Name:

_______________________________________,

____

____

____

____

____

____

____

____

____

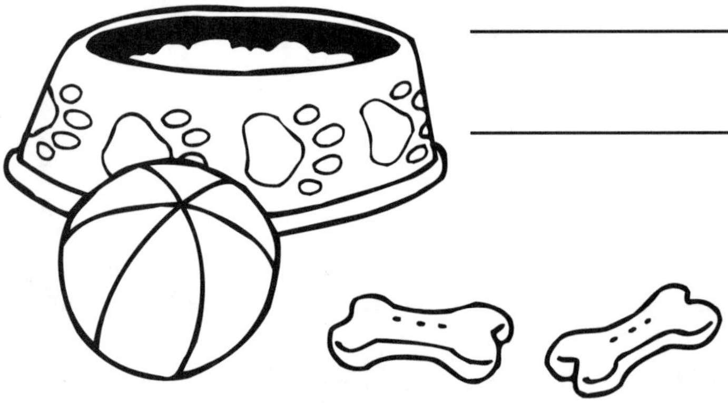

_______________________________________,

____

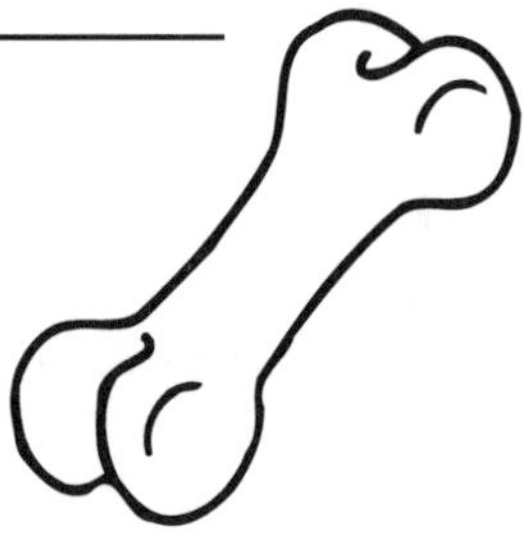

Authentic Reading Practice, Grades 1–3 • EMC 3300

Envelope Pattern

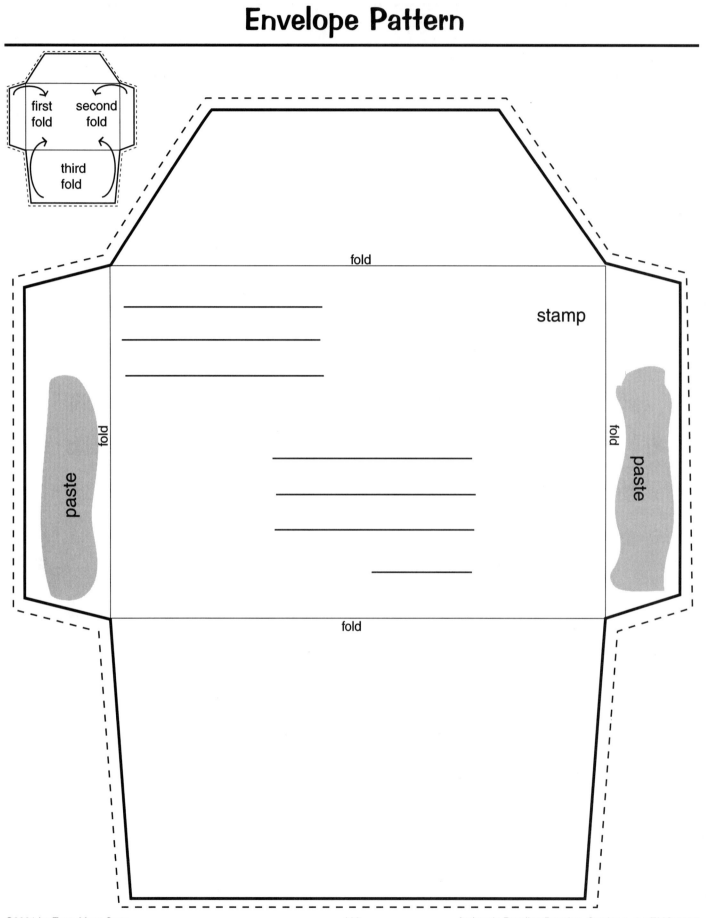

first
fold

second
fold

third
fold

fold

stamp

fold

paste

fold

paste

fold

Authentic Reading Practice, Grades 1–3 • EMC 3300

A Mail Center

Put out materials for students to write their own letters, postcards, greeting cards, invitations, etc. This mail can be delivered in class, within the school, or actually stamped and mailed from school or home.

Materials
- lined paper
- white copier paper
- stationery (pages 160 and 161 may be reproduced)
- envelopes (page 162 may be reproduced)
- pencils and ballpoint pens
- tagboard cut to 4 ¼″ x 6″ (10.6 x 15 cm) (U.S. postcard size)
- colored construction paper for cards and invitations
- marking pens
- scissors and glue

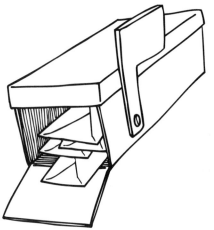

Steps to Follow

1. Provide a mailbox for in-school mail. This may be as simple as a covered box with a slit for depositing mail or a real mailbox with a flag. Arrange times for your class "mail carrier" to deliver mail to other school locations.

2. Discuss the classroom mailbox. Establish procedures for checking the box and distributing the mail. Set up standards for the letters and cards that are mailed. Require that letters sent in the mailbox meet three basic criteria:

   - Does the letter have a message?
     (This will eliminate random scribbles by younger letter writers.)

   - Does the letter tell to whom it is written?

   - Does the letter tell who sent it?

Reading Menus

Talk about motivation to read! Menus provide students with the ideal blend of real-world vocabulary and built-in interest.

ACTIVITIES

Reading a School Menu (Page 165)

Give each student a copy of a week's cafeteria menu. Use your own school's menu or reproduce page 165. Ask questions such as:

What does this menu tell us?

What can it help us decide?

Can you order special food from a school menu?

Do you have any choice of what foods you will be served?

Planning a Menu (Pages 166 and 167)

Learn about the food pyramid with the teaching ideas on page 166 and the reproducible on page 167.

Restaurant Menus (Pages 168–170)

Students will be filled with pride when they are able to order from a restaurant menu. Page 168 gives ideas, and pages 169 and 170 provide reproducibles to use.

Bay School Lunch Menu

Monday	Tuesday	Wednesday	Thursday	Friday
spaghetti	cheese sandwich	chicken nuggets	fish sticks	meat loaf
roll	carrot sticks	green beans	peas and carrots	mashed potatoes
apple	fruit cocktail	sliced bread	roll	carrot sticks
cookie	brownie	orange slices	applesauce	1/2 banana
milk or juice	milk or juice	cookie	milk or juice	milk or juice
		milk or juice		

Planning a Menu

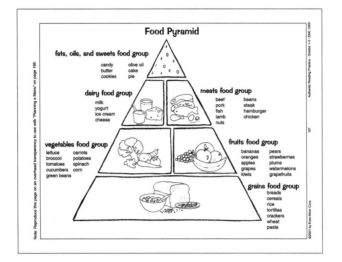

Materials
- page 167, reproduced on an overhead transparency
- drawing paper
- crayons or marking pens
- pencils
- self-sticking dots, five per student

Steps to Follow
1. Ask students, "What would you have the cafeteria serve if you could plan the menu?" Make a list of their suggestions.

2. Show the overhead transparency of the food pyramid. Read the food pyramid together. Brainstorm the foods that would be in each category.

3. Have students look at their lunch suggestions to see how healthy their choices were.

4. Have students work in pairs to plan a menu for one healthy, tasty lunch. They are to write the food name and illustrate the meal.

5. Number each menu and post them for everyone to read. Give each student five self-sticking dots. Have students put a dot on the five menus they like the best.

6. Put the winning menus together and deliver them to the school cafeteria. Write polite letters asking the cooks to consider adding one or more of the menus to the school menu.

Note: Make a transparency of this page to use with "Planning a Menu" on page 166.

Food Pyramid

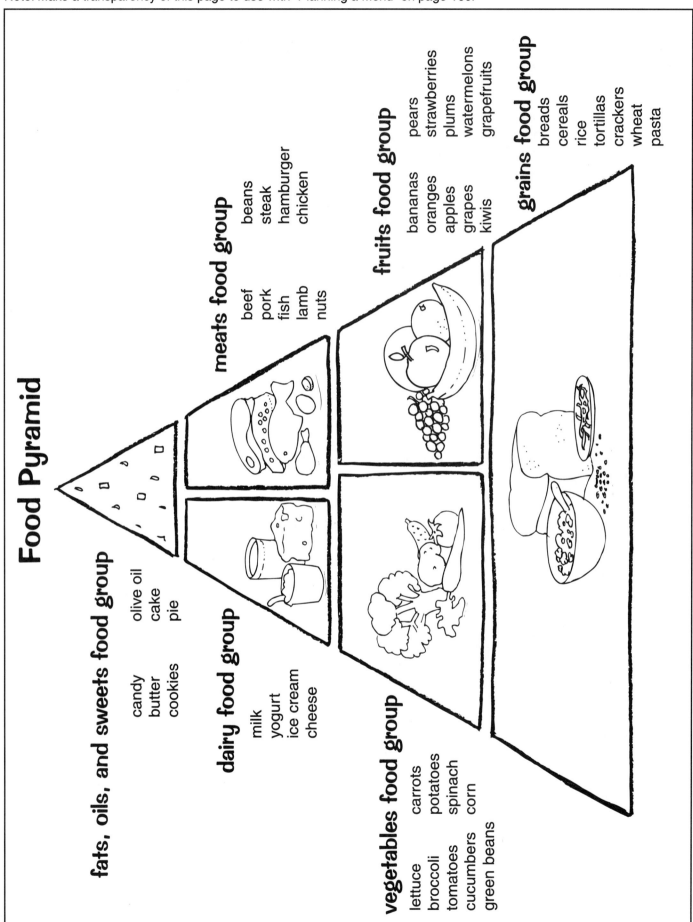

fats, oils, and sweets food group

candy
butter
cookies

olive oil
cake
pie

dairy food group

milk
yogurt
ice cream
cheese

meats food group

beef
pork
fish
lamb
nuts

beans
steak
hamburger
chicken

fruits food group

bananas
oranges
apples
grapes
kiwis

pears
strawberries
plums
watermelons
grapefruits

grains food group

breads
cereals
rice
tortillas
crackers
wheat
pasta

vegetables food group

lettuce
broccoli
tomatoes
cucumbers
green beans

carrots
potatoes
spinach
corn

Restaurant Menus

Materials
- page 169, reproduced on an overhead transparency
- page 170, reproduced for individual students
- menus of varied cuisine from local restaurants
- writing paper

Steps to Follow

1. Discuss the different types of restaurants students are familiar with.

2. Ask students to explain how they decide what to order when they eat a meal at one of these places. Do they use picture clues? Do they read a menu or a menu board? Do they have another technique?

3. Have students read the transparency. Ask what kinds of things can be ordered and how much various items cost.

4. Give each student a sheet of writing paper and have then place an "order" from the sample menu. Divide students into groups so they can share their choices.

5. Pass out real menus for small groups to explore. Allow time for the groups to examine their menus to find the following information:
   - name of the restaurants
   - kinds of foods served
   - food costs
   - business hours

6. Give each student a copy of the form on page 170. Instruct students to create an order for a breakfast, a lunch, and a dinner. Encourage them to help each other with words that are unfamiliar.

The Burger Barn

Open 5 A.M. - 12 P.M.
Breakfast served 5 A.M. - 11 A.M.
Wind-Up Wild Animal with Every Kid's Meal

Today Only 2 hamburgers for $1.00

Kid's Meal 1.99	green salad.................. 1.95
Choose from:	Caesar salad 2.25
chicken nuggets	taco salad.................... 2.50
burger	
cheeseburger	french fries
	regular 1.00
egg biscuit 99	jumbo 1.50
with sausage 1.50	onion rings 1.75
with ham...............1.50	
	cookie 75
bacon, eggs, and toast 2.95	pie 1.25
scrambled eggs and toast .1.95	ice-cream cup 75
pancakes 1.50	
	milk 65
hot dog 1.00	orange juice 85
with chili.................1.75	
with sauerkraut..........1.50	soft drink
	small 99
hamburger 99	medium 1.25
cheeseburger........1.25	large 1.59
bacon cheeseburger...2.25	
super burger 2.50	milk shake............ 1.50
chicken sandwich 2.25	vanilla
fish sandwich 2.25	chocolate
chicken nuggets	
6 ....1.00	coffee
12 ....2.00	small 75
	large 1.25

Name: _____

Place an Order

Look at your menu. You can order anything you would like. Pick what you want and write it below.

I would order this for breakfast:

_____

_____

_____

_____

I would order this for lunch:

_____

_____

_____

_____

I would order this for dinner:

_____

_____

_____

_____

Note: Make a transparency of this page to use with "Restaurant Menus" on page 168.

The Burger Barn

Open 5 A.M. - 12 P.M.
Breakfast served 5 A.M. - 11 A.M.
Wind-Up Wild Animal with
Every Kid's Meal

**Today Only
2 hamburgers
for $1.00**

Kid's Meal 1.99
Choose from:
    chicken nuggets
    burger
    cheeseburger

egg biscuit .... .99
    with sausage 1.50
    with ham.......................1.50

bacon, eggs, and toast 2.95
scrambled eggs and toast .1.95
pancakes 1.50

hot dog 1.00
    with chili.......................1.75
    with sauerkraut.............1.50

hamburger .... .99
cheeseburger....................1.25
bacon cheeseburger..........2.25
super burger 2.50
chicken sandwich 2.25
fish sandwich....................2.25
chicken nuggets
    6 ....1.00
    12 ....2.00

green salad.................. 1.95
Caesar salad 2.25
taco salad 2.50

french fries
    regular................... 1.00
    jumbo 1.50
onion rings.................. 1.75

cookie .... .75
pie 1.25
ice-cream cup .... .75

milk .... .65
orange juice .... .85

soft drink
    small......................... .99
    medium 1.25
    large 1.59

milk shake.................... 1.50
    vanilla
    chocolate

coffee
    small......................... .75
    large 1.25

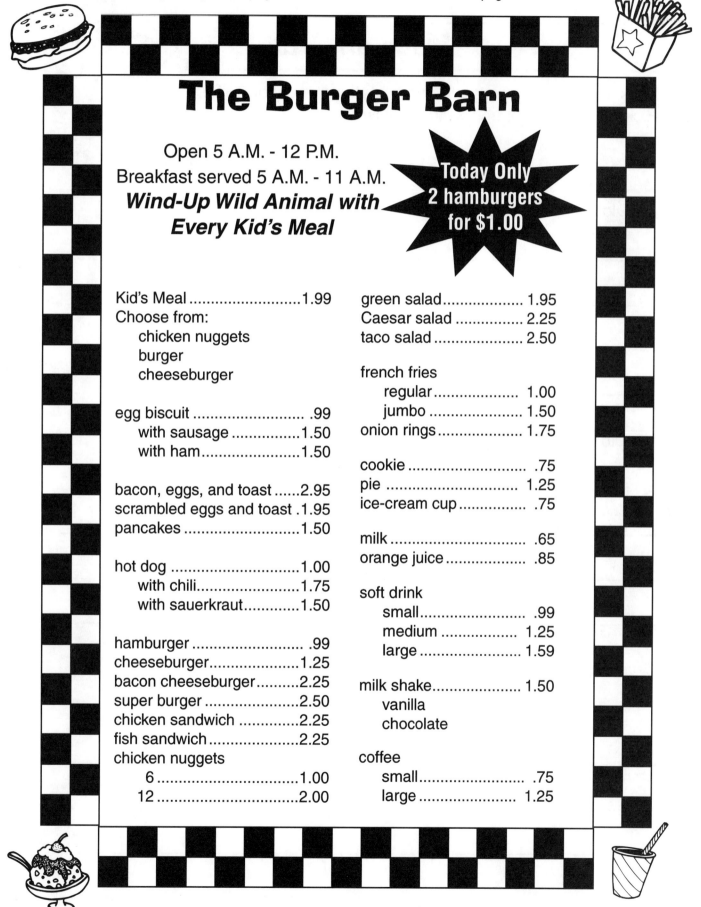

Authentic Reading Practice, Grades 1–3 • EMC 3300

Note: Reproduce this form to use with "Restaurant Menus" on page 168.

Name:

Place an Order

Look at your menu. You can order anything you would like.
Pick what you want and write it below.

I would order this for breakfast:

_____

_____

_____

_____

I would order this for lunch:

_____

_____

_____

_____

I would order this for dinner:

_____

_____

_____

_____

Everyday Reading Skills Checklist ✓

	Students' Names								
Reads and analyzes information on containers, labels, and price tags									
Reads positional words									
Follows simple maps, charts, and signs to locate a destination									
Knows the parts of a friendly letter									
Reads and addresses an envelope									
Reads and writes friendly letters									
Reads and writes invitations									
Reads a school lunch menu									
Reads the food pyramid and uses it to plan a menu									
Reads restaurant menus to choose a meal									

Part 4

Reading at the Supermarket

Food is a basic human need. Think how empowered your students will feel when they have the reading skills to successfully navigate a supermarket, read directions and food labels, and make appropriate choices!

Going to the Supermarket

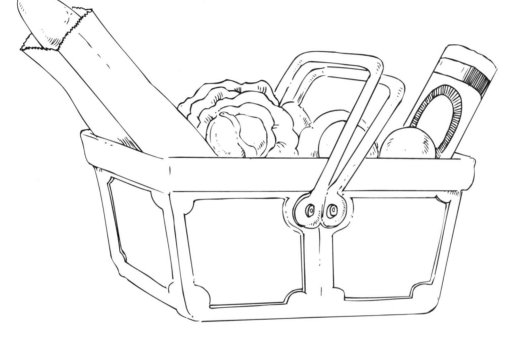

This section contains some tips for getting ready to teach this topic and then demonstrates that there's a lot of reading to do even before starting to shop.

ACTIVITIES

Getting Started (Pages 174–176)
Read the preparation tips for the section and then reproduce the supermarket logbook cover and logbook entry page.

Outside the Supermarket (Pages 177–180)
Follow the lessons on page 177 to practice reading words outside the supermarket.

The Store Directory (Pages 181 and 182)
A directory lists items found in the supermarket and tells where they are found. Follow the teaching ideas on page 181, using the reproducible sample directory on page 182.

Getting Started

Preparation

1. Collect empty food boxes and containers, supermarket fliers, advertisements, and paper and plastic bags.

2. Contact local supermarkets to find out what type of support they are willing to provide. Ask about field trips, speakers who will come to school, samples of promotional materials, tours of their operations, and try-out-a-job partnerships.

Plan for Hands-on Activities

1. Make your reading real by using actual containers, advertisements, coupons, receipts, etc. The activities in this book provide instruction. Be sure to follow up with practice reading real items.

2. Visit local markets several times. Set a purpose for each trip and be sure to follow up when you return to school (a great opportunity to write thank-you letters).

3. Set up a "minimarket" in your classroom. See pages 220 and 221 for details.

Make a Supermarket Logbook

Materials
• cover illustration on page 175, reproduced for each student
• logbook page on page 176, reproduced in quantity
• hole punch
• binder rings, yarn, or paper fasteners

Logbook Activities

1. Make logbook entries following any of the activities in this section. Students may summarize what they did and what they learned.

2. Report on field trips taken to local markets.

3. When questions come up in class discussions, have students respond by writing their answers in their logbooks before answering in class.

4. Have students describe the responsibilities of supermarket employees. Encourage them to point out the skills that the employees use in their work.

5. Write about the supermarket of the future. What will it look like? Will the amount of print in the store change? Why or why not?

6. Develop a new section for a supermarket. What things would be included in this section? How would they be displayed?

7. Think of a name for a supermarket. Tell why the name would attract customers. Develop a logo for the new supermarket.

by Sandy Lucido

My Supermarket Log

by _____

Supermarket
Log

_____

_____

_____

_____

_____

_____

_____

_____

_____

_____

_____

_____

_____

_____

Outside the Supermarket

From the Parking Lot

Even before you go into the store, you begin reading. You might see the name of the store, featured sale items, directions for parking, vending machines, newspaper racks, pay telephones, and directions for entering the store.

- Reproduce the supermarket illustration on page 178 on an overhead transparency. Read the words and phrases together.

- Reproduce the phrase cards on pages 179 and 180 for reading practice. Ask students to tell where these phrases might be found.

Reading the Shopping Cart

These days you generally find the shopping carts lined up outside the market. A shopping cart is yet another reading experience. You may find the name of the store, advertisements, a store directory, a warning to not leave children in the cart unattended, etc.

- Go to the market and take photographs or slides of the print on shopping carts. Share these with the class.

- On your field trip to a market, take time to read the print on the cart.

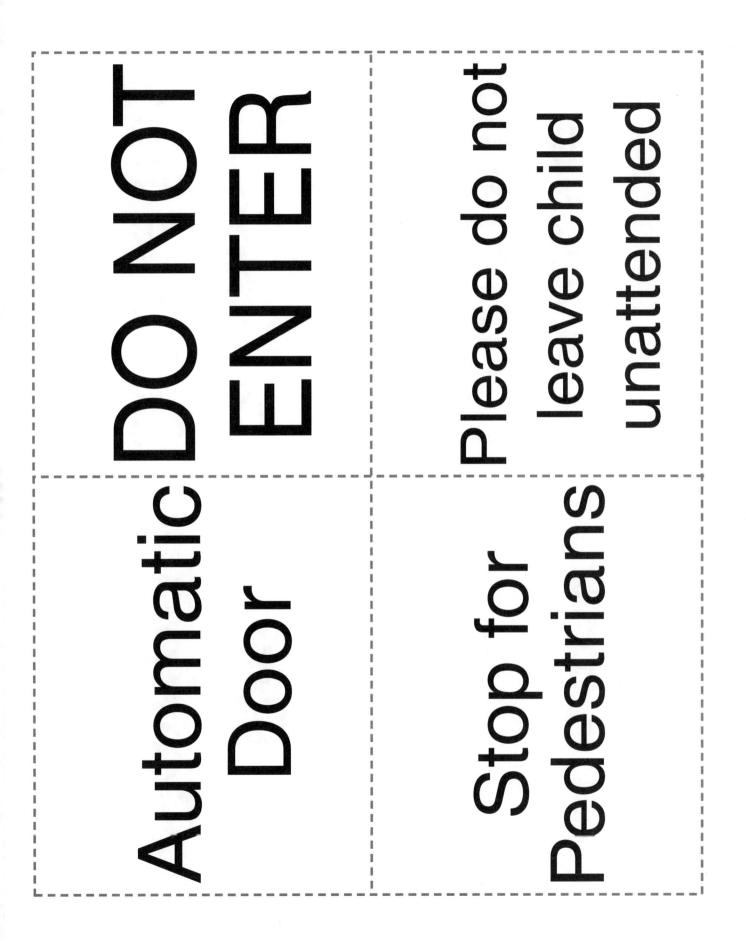

DO NOT ENTER

Automatic Door

Please do not leave child unattended

Stop for Pedestrians

Authentic Reading Practice, Grades 1–3 • EMC 3300

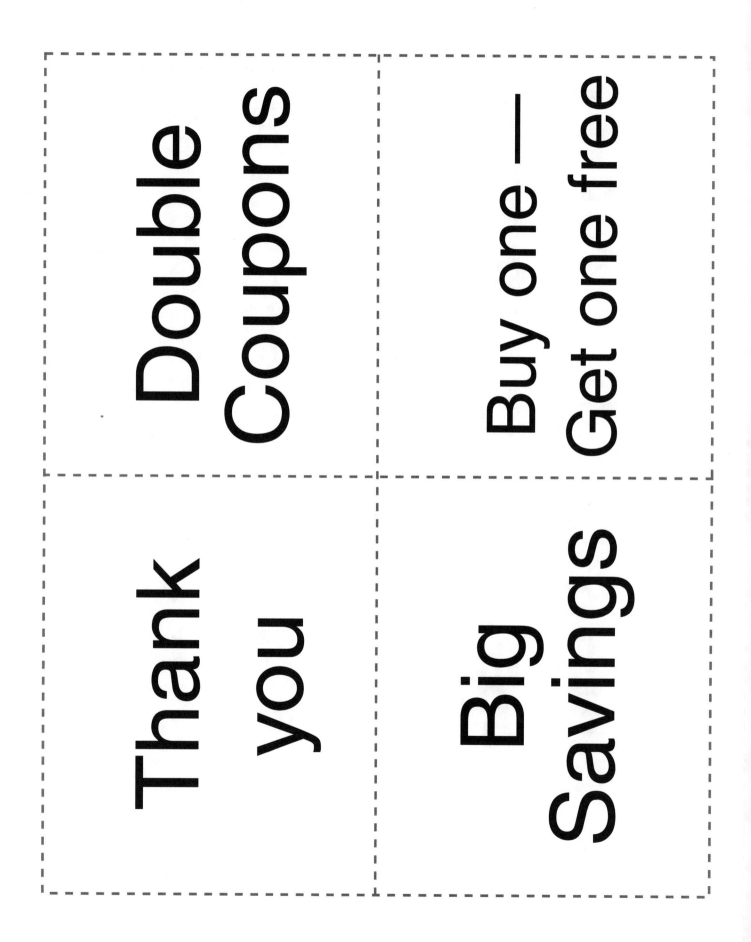

Double
Coupons

Buy one —
Get one free

Thank
you

Big
Savings

Authentic Reading Practice, Grades 1–3 • EMC 3300

The Store Directory

A Sample Directory

Make an overhead transparency of the sample directory on page 182. Use it to practice finding the location of specific items in the supermarket. Ask questions such as:

How are the items on the directory organized?

Is every item carried in the store listed?

Are specific brand names listed?

What would you look under to locate plastic spoons? A Snickers® bar? Some Cheerios®?

What can you do if you can't find the specific item on the directory?

A Real Directory

When the class visits a local supermarket, be sure to take time to find the store directory and use it to locate specific items.

- In advance of the field trip, divide students into small groups. Let each group decide on items to locate. Students will need to put the specific items into a general category listed on the directory. (For example, pork chops would be found by looking under meats.)

- During the field trip, each group determines the location of their items, goes to that area of the store, and locates the items.

Note: Make a transparency of this page to use with "A Sample Directory" on page 181.

Store Directory

Aluminum Foil	aisle 15	Light Bulbs	aisle 18
Aspirin	aisle 22	Macaroni	aisle 4
Baby Food	aisle 13	Marshmallows	aisle 10
Bags, plastic	aisle 15	Meat, canned	aisle 9
Baking powder	aisle 11	Nuts	aisle 11
Beans	aisle 9	Oil, motor	aisle 18
Butter	dairy case	Oil, salad	aisle 11
Cake Mix	aisle 11	Paper Goods	aisle 15
Candy	aisle 7	Pickles	aisle 8
Cat Food	aisle 16	Picnic Supplies	aisle 15
Cereal	aisle 10	Pizza, frozen	aisle 1
Coffee	aisle 10	Popcorn	aisle 6
Cookies	aisle 7	Potato Chips	aisle 6
Crackers	aisle 5	Salad Dressing	aisle 8
Detergents	aisle 14	Shampoo	aisle 23
Dog Food	aisle 16	Shortening	aisle 11
Eggs	dairy case	Soft Drinks	aisle 12
Fish, canned	aisle 9	Soup	aisle 9
Fish, frozen	aisle 3	Spices	aisle 11
Frozen Foods	aisles 1,2,3	Sugar	aisle 11
Honey	aisle 8	Tea	aisle 10
Ice Cream	aisle 2	Tomato Sauce	aisle 9
Insect Spray	aisle 18	Toothpaste	aisle 23
Juice, canned	aisle 13	Tortillas	aisle 4
Juice, frozen	aisle 3	Tuna	aisle 9
Juice, refrigerated	dairy case	Yeast	aisle 11
Laundry Soaps	aisle 14		

©2001 by Evan-Moor Corp.   182   Authentic Reading Practice - Grades 1-3 - EMC 3300

Store Directory

Aluminum Foil	*aisle 15*	Light Bulbs	*aisle 18*
Aspirin	*aisle 22*	Macaroni	*aisle 4*
Baby Food	*aisle 13*	Marshmallows	*aisle 10*
Bags, plastic	*aisle 15*	Meat, canned	*aisle 9*
Baking Powder	*aisle 11*	Nuts	*aisle 11*
Beans	*aisle 9*	Oil, motor	*aisle 18*
Butter	*dairy case*	Oil, salad	*aisle 11*
Cake Mix	*aisle 11*	Paper Goods	*aisle 15*
Candy	*aisle 7*	Pickles	*aisle 8*
Cat Food	*aisle 16*	Picnic Supplies	*aisle 15*
Cereal	*aisle 10*	Pizza, frozen	*aisle 1*
Coffee	*aisle 10*	Popcorn	*aisle 6*
Cookies	*aisle 7*	Potato Chips	*aisle 6*
Crackers	*aisle 5*	Salad Dressing	*aisle 8*
Detergents	*aisle 14*	Shampoo	*aisle 23*
Dog Food	*aisle 16*	Shortening	*aisle 11*
Eggs	*dairy case*	Soft Drinks	*aisle 12*
Fish, canned	*aisle 9*	Soup	*aisle 9*
Fish, frozen	*aisle 3*	Spices	*aisle 11*
Frozen Foods	*aisles 1, 2, 3*	Sugar	*aisle 11*
Honey	*aisle 8*	Tea	*aisle 10*
Ice Cream	*aisle 2*	Tomato Sauce	*aisle 9*
Insect Spray	*aisle 18*	Toothpaste	*aisle 23*
Juice, canned	*aisle 13*	Tortillas	*aisle 4*
Juice, frozen	*aisle 3*	Tuna	*aisle 9*
Juice, refrigerated	*dairy case*	Yeast	*aisle 11*
Laundry Soaps	*aisle 14*		

Sections of a Supermarket

Produce

Canned Goods

Frozen Foods

Meat Department

Bakery

Dairy

Spices

Cereal

In a supermarket, similar products are placed together in sections. Many different kinds of cereal are in the breakfast food section. All the fresh produce is in one area. The paper products form another section.

ACTIVITIES

Which Product Doesn't Belong? (Page 184)
Reproduce page 184 on an overhead transparency or for individual students. Have students choose the product in each section that does not belong.

Where Can You Find It? (Pages 185–190)
This activity helps students learn to read the names of supermarket items and to categorize them by store section.

Supermarket Sections Activities (Pages 191–202)
The reproducibles on these pages provide lots of practice reading information such as that found in various sections of the market. Help students develop strategies for using context to figure out new words. Bring in real examples and apply the strategies you developed as you read them.

Name:

Which Product Doesn't Belong?

The night stockers had some trouble last night. Help Mr. Thomas find their mistakes. Identify the item that doesn't belong on each shelf. Make an **X** on it to show that it has been shelved incorrectly.

Tell where each misplaced item belongs.

 _____

_____

 _____

_____

Where Can You Find It?

Materials
- supermarket section signs on pages 186–188
- forms for product word cards on page 189
- product word lists on page 190

Preparing the Activity
1. Reproduce the supermarket section signs. Add color if desired. Glue the signs to tagboard, laminate, and cut apart.

2. Make 12 copies of the word card forms on page 189.

3. Write the products listed on page 190 on the word cards (one sheet of eight products for each of the 12 supermarket sections). This is your master copy.

4. Reproduce one set of the 12 finished word card pages. Glue the pages to tagboard and laminate.

5. Cut the cards apart.

Conducting the Activity
1. Display the 12 supermarket section signs.

2. Mix up the product word cards and distribute them to students. (You may want to do only a portion of the cards at a time.)

3. Students read the cards and place them in the correct section of the supermarket.

4. Record the way the class divided the products. When you take a field trip, compare this to the way the products are actually categorized in the store.

Note: Put the cards in envelopes and reuse them as a center activity.

Note: Reproduce pages 186–188 to use with "Where Can You Find It?" on page 185.

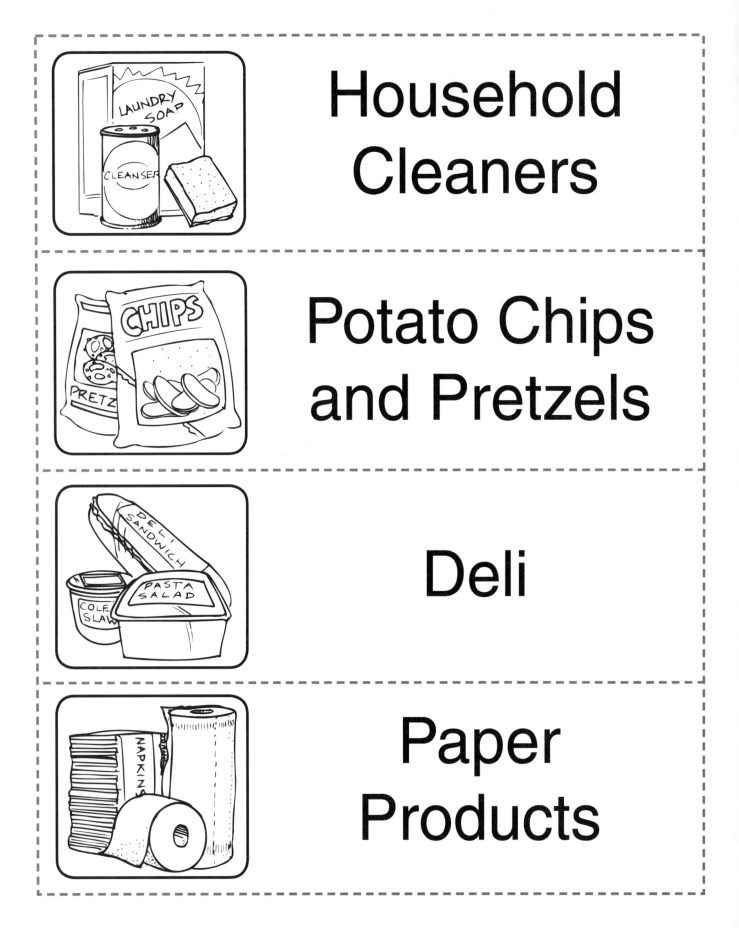

Household Cleaners

Potato Chips and Pretzels

Deli

Paper Products

Dairy Foods

Bakery

Crackers and Cookies

Baby Needs

 Authentic Reading Practice, Grades 1–3 • EMC 3300

Produce

Baking Needs

Canned Goods

Meat

Note: Reproduce 12 copies of this page to use with "Where Can You Find It?" on page 185.

Forms for Product Word Cards

Authentic Reading Practice, Grades 1–3 • EMC 3300

Words for Product Word Cards

Here are suggested products for making cards to be used in "Where Can You Find It?" (page 185). After reproducing 12 copies of page 189, write the name of one product in each box to create the cards.

Household Cleaners
- liquid detergent
- powdered cleanser
- disinfectant spray
- glass cleaner
- all purpose cleanser
- hard water stain remover
- steel wool pads
- mildew remover

Potato Chips and Pretzels
- cheese puffs
- potato chips
- corn chips
- tortilla chips
- pretzel sticks
- snack mix
- Cracker Jack®
- popcorn

Paper Products
- facial tissue
- toilet paper
- paper towels
- paper napkins
- paper plates
- Styrofoam® cups
- lunch sacks
- table covers

Crackers and Cookies
- Fig Newtons®
- Saltines® crackers
- Triscuits®
- animal cookies
- vanilla wafers
- Ginger Snaps®
- shortbread
- Ry-Krisp®

Deli
- sliced turkey breast
- pastrami
- fresh sliced swiss cheese
- macaroni salad
- salami
- cheese balls
- potato salad
- bologna

Bakery
- dinner rolls
- bagels
- assorted muffins
- hamburger buns
- angel food cake
- crushed wheat bread
- coffee cake
- bread sticks

Baby Needs
- disposable diapers
- baby wipes
- baby powder
- turkey and rice baby food
- rice and banana cereal
- baby formula
- bibs
- Zwieback Toast®

Dairy Products
- margarine
- buttermilk
- yogurt
- cottage cheese
- ricotta
- chocolate milk
- sour cream
- whipping cream

Canned Goods
- SpaghettiOs®
- tuna
- chili con carne
- tomato sauce
- crushed pineapple
- cream-style corn
- fruit cocktail
- French-style beans

Baking Needs
- unbleached flour
- cornbread mix
- lemon supreme cake mix
- chocolate chips
- corn starch
- granulated sugar
- baking soda
- active dry yeast

Produce
- lettuce
- strawberries
- carrots
- potatoes
- bananas
- onions
- asparagus
- parsley

Meat
- chicken thighs
- fresh bratwurst
- thick-sliced bacon
- lean ground beef
- boned turkey breast
- hamburger
- round steak
- leg of lamb

Name:

The Produce Section

The produce section of the supermarket is filled with fresh fruits and vegetables.

Read the information on this package.
Answer the questions to show that you understand what the package says.

1. How much does each package weigh?

_____

2. Where were the carrots shipped from?

_____

3. What do you have to do to the carrots before you eat them? How do you know?

_____

Name:

Reading the Produce Department

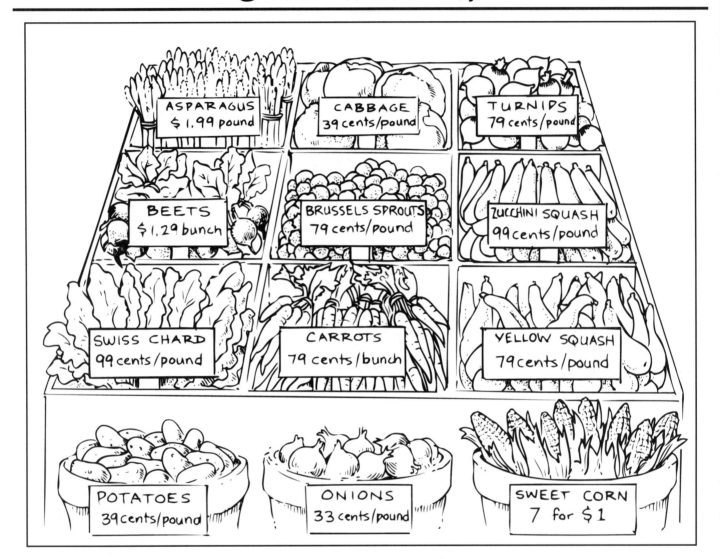

ASPARAGUS $1.99 pound

CABBAGE 39 cents/pound

TURNIPS 79 cents/pound

BEETS $1.29 bunch

BRUSSELS SPROUTS 79 cents/pound

ZUCCHINI SQUASH 99 cents/pound

SWISS CHARD 99 cents/pound

CARROTS 79 cents/bunch

YELLOW SQUASH 79 cents/pound

POTATOES 39 cents/pound

ONIONS 33 cents/pound

SWEET CORN 7 for $1

1. What types of squash are for sale? What is the difference in price?

_____

2. What root vegetables are in this produce department?

_____

_____

3. What leafy vegetables are in this department?

_____

The Meat Department

The meat department in most supermarkets is a series of refrigerated display units where fresh and frozen meats are available.

Practice reading the labels of several different kinds of meat. Tell what you know about the meat after reading the labels.

The Bakery

The supermarket bakery contains bread, rolls, cookies, cakes, and many other fresh-baked treats.

Read these labels and match them with the bakery items on the right that they name.

Baked-to-Order

Many supermarket customers order cakes for special occasions. The baker makes and decorates the cakes according to the instructions on the order form. Read this order form and then complete it to order a cake.

Forest Market Bakery

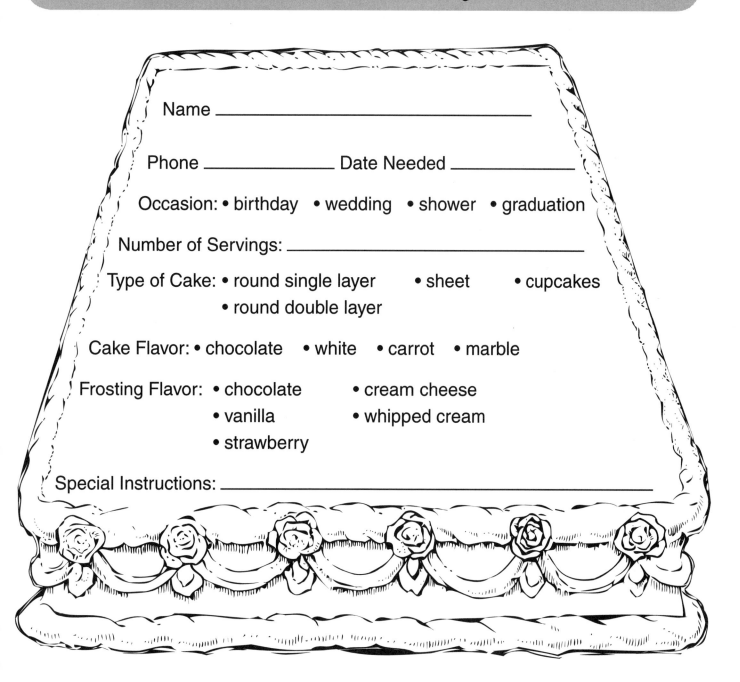

Name _____

Phone _____ Date Needed _____

Occasion: • birthday • wedding • shower • graduation

Number of Servings: _____

Type of Cake: • round single layer   • sheet   • cupcakes
               • round double layer

Cake Flavor: • chocolate • white • carrot • marble

Frosting Flavor: • chocolate   • cream cheese
                 • vanilla   • whipped cream
                 • strawberry

Special Instructions: _____

Name:

Frozen Foods

Any item that is sold while it is frozen is usually found in the frozen food section of the supermarket. Ice cream, frozen fruits and vegetables, prepared dinners, pizzas, and juices fill the freezers.

1. Read the labels on the freezer case.
2. Cut out the food names below.
3. Paste the food in the right freezer case.

chopped spinach

chocolate pound cake

pumpkin pie

frozen pot pie

ice-cream sandwich

baby early peas in
butter sauce

popsicle

lasagna with
meat sauce

peach cobbler

raspberry sorbet

pizza

stir-fry vegetables

The Dairy Section

The dairy section in the supermarket is another refrigerated section. Milk, cheeses, and eggs must be kept cool so that they will stay fresh.

Dairy products spoil if they are left on the shelf for too long. Each dairy container has a date on it that tells by when the product must be sold.

1. Circle the "sell by" date on each container.
2. Pretend it is July first. Make an X on the item you would be likely to see in the market.
3. Look for the "sell by" date on dairy section products you have at home.

Canned Goods

Many products in the supermarket come in cans. There are canned vegetables and fruits, sauces, and other prepared foods.

The labels on the cans in the supermarket are full of information. Read the label below and then answer the questions to show that you understand what you read.

Directions: Mix soup and one can of water. Heat on stove, stirring constantly. Or microwave on **High** **2 1/2** minutes or until hot.

Nutritional Facts
Serving size: 1 cup (240 ml)
Servings: about 2½
Calories.............................75
Fat Cal. 25

Satisfaction guaranteed or your money back.
If you have questions, call 1-800-111-1111.

BlueBells
Condensed Soup
Chicken Noodle
SOUP

1. How many servings does this can make?

_____

2. What are the directions for preparing the soup?

_____

_____

3. If you are not satisfied with the quality of the soup, what can you do?

_____

Note: Reproduce this page and page 201 on overhead transparencies. Read the directions with the class and discuss the information read.

Name:

The Cereal Row at the Supermarket

The supermarket has so many different kinds of cereal that they fill up almost a whole section. Cereal boxes, like the cans in the supermarket, are filled with important information.

front of cereal box

Harvest Pride
Instant Oatmeal
• CHOLESTEROL FREE •
10 1.23 oz. packets
Net. wt. 12.3 oz. 350 g
GOOD SOURCE OF ENERGY!
See side panel for nutrition facts

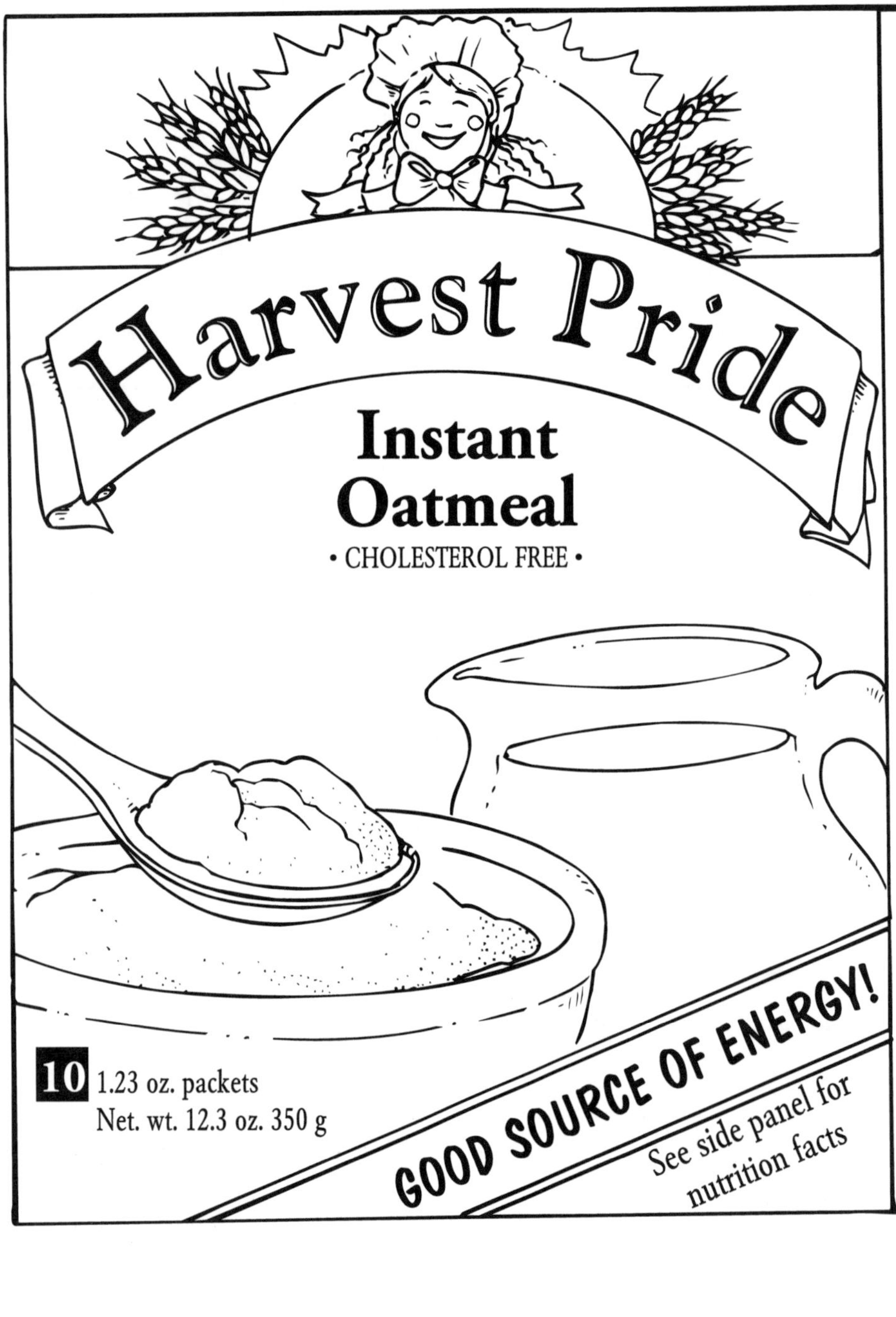

side panel of cereal box

Nutritional Facts

Serving Size: 1 packet

Servings Per Container: 10

Amount Per Serving

Calories 130 Calories from Fat 20

	% Daily Value
Total Fat 2 g	3%
Cholesterol 0 mg	0%
Sodium 150 mg	6%
Total Carbohydrate 27 g	9%
Protein 3 g	*
Vitamin A	20%
Vitamin C	0%
Calcium	10%
Iron	30%
Thiamin	20%
Riboflavin	10%
Niacin	15%
Vitamin B_6	15%
Folate	25%

* no minimum daily requirement established.

back of cereal box   *side panel of cereal box*

Harvest Pride

Help your family get the energy they need. Grains are the foundation of a nutritious diet. You should have 6 servings a day. Start your family's day with the whole-grain goodness of instant oatmeal.

Ingredients: Whole grain rolled oats, sugar, soybean oil, whey, flavored fruit pieces

Directions: Make with boiling water.

Empty packet into bowl.

Add 1/3 cup boiling water; stir.

Microwave Directions:

Empty packet into microwave-safe bowl.

Add ½ cup water or milk. Microwave on HIGH 1 to 2 minutes. Stir.

Note: Reproduce this page for individual students to design their own cereal box.

Name:

Invent Your Own

Design a cereal box for a new cereal. Give the cereal a name. Write the information on the box that would tell consumers what they need to know about the cereal.

front or back of cereal box   *side panel of cereal box*

                   Authentic Reading Practice, Grades 1–3 • EMC 3300

Shopping Lists

Shopping lists are essential. Without a list, one is likely to forget an important item, necessitating another trip to the store. In this section, students practice reading and writing shopping lists.

ACTIVITIES

Which Shopping List? (Page 204)
Students read each shopping list and match it to the correct group of items pictured.

Using a Shopping List (Pages 205–207)
Students "shop" for the items that are on their lists. Start collecting containers if you decide to use the ready-made shopping lists on page 206, or use the form on page 207 to create your own lists.

Writing a Shopping List (Page 208)
Students read the recipe on page 208 and write a shopping list for the ingredients they will need.

Name:

Which Shopping List?

Cut out each list below and paste it beside the picture that shows those items.

loaf of bread	loaf of bread	eggs	can of soup
milk	can of tuna	orange juice	chips
cottage cheese	lettuce	bananas	chicken
jam	flour	milk	apple
cookies	nuts	strawberries	honey

 Authentic Reading Practice, Grades 1–3 • EMC 3300

Using a Shopping List

Materials
- shopping lists on page 206, reproduced for students, or your own shopping lists made using the form on page 207
- baskets or shopping bags with handles

Steps to Follow

1. Display the supermarket items (or containers) from the lists on page 206, or use items of your own choosing.

2. Divide the class into small groups. Give each group a basket or bag and a different shopping list.

3. Groups read the shopping list together to make sure that they agree on what items are to be "purchased."

4. Groups choose one student to shop for the items on the list. Allow the shoppers from no more than three groups to shop at the same time.

5. When the shoppers return to the group, the group evaluates whether all the correct items were picked.

6. Groups switch lists with another group and choose a new shopper.

7. Continue until all students have had the chance to be the shopper.

Note: Reproduce this page and page 207 to use with "Using a Shopping List" on page 205.

My Shopping List	My Shopping List
sponge	dried spaghetti
Fig Newtons®	chocolate cake mix
tomato juice	bread sticks
cornbread mix	paper plates
chili con carne	French-cut green beans
fruit cocktail	Cracker Jack®
pita bread	paper cups
pretzel sticks	bar soap

My Shopping List	My Shopping List
sour cream	salt
salsa	baby powder
SpaghettiOs®	Triscuits®
nonfat milk	margarine
jar of baby food	cream-style corn
liquid hand soap	paper napkins
facial tissue	hamburger buns
boxed juice drink	canned tuna

My Shopping List	My Shopping List
canned peaches	cereal
kidney beans	potato chips
dry soap mix	Saltines® crackers
vanilla wafers	rice
pickles	tomato sauce
mustard	paper towels
popcorn	yogurt
Mortons® salt	sugar

©2001 by Evan-Moor Corp.   206   Authentic Reading Practice, Grades 1–3 • EMC 3300

My Shopping List	My Shopping List

My Shopping List	My Shopping List

My Shopping List	My Shopping List

©2001 by Evan-Moor Corp.   207   Authentic Reading Practice, Grades 1–3 • EMC 3300

My Shopping List

sponge
Fig Newtons®
tomato juice
cornbread mix
chili con carne
fruit cocktail
pita bread
pretzel sticks

My Shopping List

dried spaghetti
chocolate cake mix
bread sticks
paper plates
French-cut green beans
Cracker Jack®
paper cups
bar soap

My Shopping List

sour cream
salsa
SpaghettiOs®
nonfat milk
jar of baby food
liquid hand soap
facial tissue
boxed juice drink

My Shopping List

salt
baby powder
Triscuits®
margarine
cream-style corn
paper napkins
hamburger buns
canned tuna

My Shopping List

canned peaches
kidney beans
dry soup mix
vanilla wafers
pickles
mustard
popcorn
Mortons® salt

My Shopping List

cereal
potato chips
Saltines® crackers
rice
tomato sauce
paper towels
yogurt
sugar

My Shopping List

My Shopping List

My Shopping List

My Shopping List

My Shopping List

My Shopping List

Note: Reproduce this page to use with "Writing a Shopping List" on page 203.

Stuffed Apple Rings

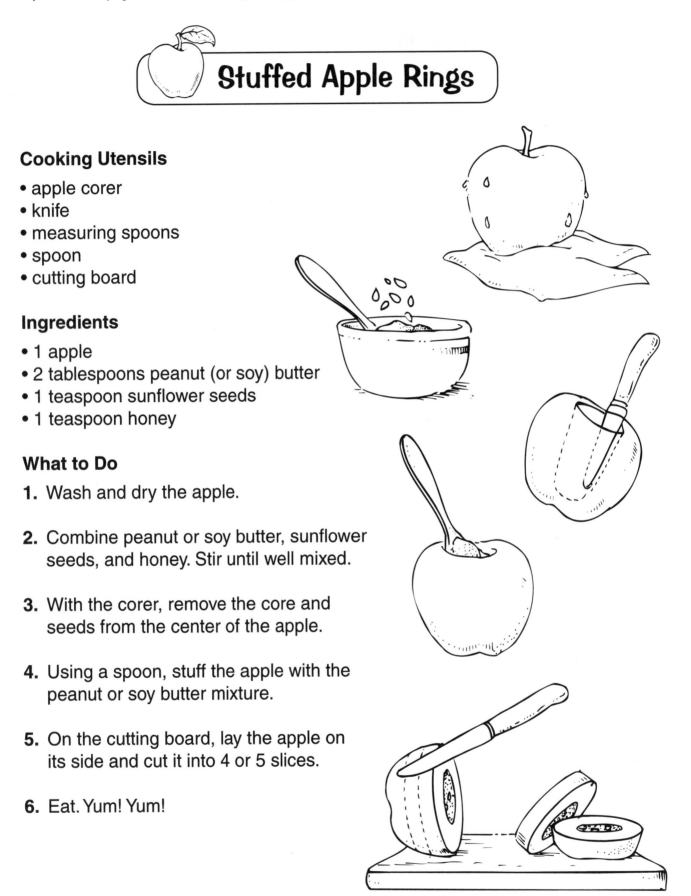

Cooking Utensils

- apple corer
- knife
- measuring spoons
- spoon
- cutting board

Ingredients

- 1 apple
- 2 tablespoons peanut (or soy) butter
- 1 teaspoon sunflower seeds
- 1 teaspoon honey

What to Do

1. Wash and dry the apple.

2. Combine peanut or soy butter, sunflower seeds, and honey. Stir until well mixed.

3. With the corer, remove the core and seeds from the center of the apple.

4. Using a spoon, stuff the apple with the peanut or soy butter mixture.

5. On the cutting board, lay the apple on its side and cut it into 4 or 5 slices.

6. Eat. Yum! Yum!

Supermarket Coupons and Advertising

The activities in this section help students learn how coupons work and how to read supermarket ads.

ACTIVITIES

Reading and Using Coupons (Pages 210 and 211)
Use the sample coupons provided, or bring in real ones to teach students how to understand what coupons are and how to read them.

Advertising and Comparison Shopping (Pages 212–214)
It's a lot of fun to read supermarket ads and decide where to get the best buys!

Reading and Using Coupons

Materials
- sample coupons on page 211, reproduced on an overhead transparency
- a variety of real coupons from your local newspaper, advertising supplements, or magazines—enough for one per student
- chart paper
- marking pen
- computer with scanner and audio recording capabilities (optional)

Steps to Follow

1. Make a chart listing the important things to look for on a coupon. Ask questions such as:

   What product is this coupon for?

   How many items do you have to buy to get the discount?

   How much is the discount?

   Is there an expiration date?

   Can you use more than one coupon?

2. Read the coupons on the overhead transparency and use the chart to discuss the important components of each coupon.

3. Give a real coupon to each student.

4. Have students work in pairs to read the coupons.

5. Optional: Scan the coupons into your computer and record students reading them. Share this audio-coupon book with a kindergarten class. What fun for younger students to hear environmental print read aloud for them!

Follow-up

1. Use the real coupons to discount the prices in your class minimarket.

2. Before a field trip to a supermarket, let students choose a few coupons to use in buying items at the store.

Regular Price 27¢
Coupon Price 23¢
Savings 4¢

Note: Make a transparency of this page to use with "Reading and Using Coupons" on page 210.

Reading and Using Coupons

Any Store Coupon Effective thru May 21, 2005

Dairy Delight
- 8 Oz. • Low Fat
- Selected Varieties

Dairy Delight
Red Raspberry Yogurt

3 $1 FOR

SAVE 20¢ on 3

Limit 3 With Coupon.
Limit 1 Coupon Per Customer.

Any Store Coupon Effective thru May 21, 2005

Fruit Punch
12 Oz.
Rhonda Lee

3 $1 FOR

SAVE 50¢ on 3

Fruit Punch

Rhonda Lee

Limit 6 With Coupon.
Limit 1 Coupon Per Customer.

Any Store Coupon Effective thru May 21, 2005

LUIGI'S
Spaghetti Curlys

LUIGI'S

Pasta
14.75 to 15 Oz.
10 Varieties

SAVE 58¢ on 2

2 $1 FOR

Limit 2 With Coupon.
Limit 1 Coupon Per Customer.

Any Store Coupon Effective thru May 21, 2005

Rhonda Lee Bread
24 Oz.
White

WHITE BREAD
Rhonda Lee

79¢

SAVE 20¢ ea.

Limit 1 With Coupon.
Limit 1 Coupon Per Customer.

Advertising and Comparison Shopping

Materials
- sample advertisement on page 213, reproduced on an overhead transparency
- comparison shopping record sheet on page 214, reproduced for each student
- supermarket fliers
- chart paper
- marking pen

Steps to Follow

1. Show the overhead transparency of the sample supermarket ad.

2. Ask students to identify what they recognize as "ad" words. Record these words on a chart to make an Ad Word Bank.

3. Practice reading supermarket fliers. Partners or small groups might do this, with each student having a copy of the same flier. The picture clues and familiar environmental print provide valuable context for reading new words.

4. Assign pairs of students ad sections from different supermarkets. Have them look for items of the same type (e.g., spaghetti sauces) and compare prices.

5. Each student should record the pair's findings on a copy of page 214.

Sample Advertisement

Orville Matson Wieners
• 1 lb Package • Great for the Grill
• *SAVE up to 60¢ ea*

1⁹⁹ ea

FOREST GROCERY

Everyday Low Prices

The Best Quality

The Biggest Savings

Best Buy Cheddar Cheese
• Approx. 24 oz.
• or Monterey Jack

2⁴⁹ lb

Boneless Barbeque Steaks
• Crossrib • Value Pack—3 lbs or More
• USDA Select Beef

VALU PACK

1⁷⁹ lb

Crispy Corn Flakes
• 18 oz.
• *SAVE up to $1.00*

crispy CORN FLAKES

2⁹⁹

Got moo juice?

Large Cantaloupes
sweet

Large Bell Peppers
green

69¢ lb

2 $1 FOR

Note: Reproduce this page to use with "Advertising and Comparison Shopping" on page 212.

Comparison Shopping

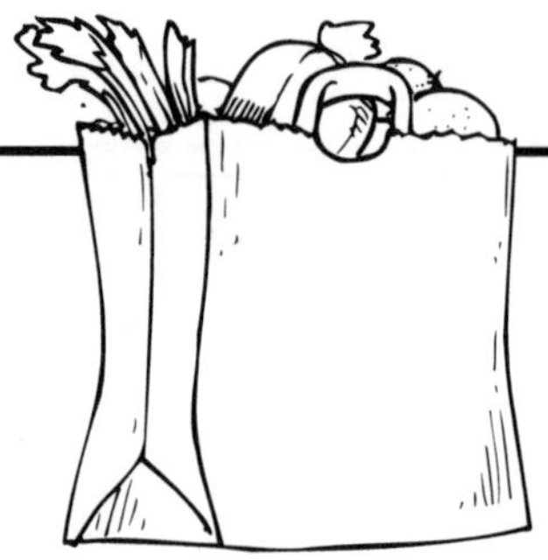

Record Sheet

Some things to consider:

- Is one product larger than another?
- Is there a cost difference?

	Product 1	Product 2
Name:		
Size:		
Price:		

Which product is the best buy? Explain why you think as you do.

____

____

	Product 1	Product 2
Name:		
Size:		
Price:		

Which product is the best buy? Explain why you think as you do.

____

____

Checking Out

Now students will need to pay for their purchases and make sure the receipt is correct. Here's some practice doing those tasks.

ACTIVITIES

Reading and Writing a Check (Page 216)
Following a model, students practice filling out a check to pay for groceries. Reproduce page 216 on an overhead transparency and for individual students. Have students read the words on the check and discuss what each section means. Discuss how the filled-in sample has been done. Demonstrate how to fill in the blanks on the bottom check. Have students fill in their own copies.

Reading Supermarket Receipts (Pages 217 and 218)
Use the sample receipt reproducible on page 218 as you conduct the activities on page 217.

Note: Reproduce this page to use with "Reading and Writing a Check" on pages 215 and 220.

Name:

Sample Checks

Sally Student
Room 7
Bayview School

0001

Date 2-5-02

12-34/1112
111222555

Pay to the Order of Forest Market

$ 8.50

Eight and 50/100 Dollars

Your Bank
Main Street
Your Town, USA 91234

For Snacks for trip

Sally Student

0001

Date ____________

12-34/1112
111222555

Pay to the Order of ____________

$

____________ Dollars

Your Bank
Main Street
Your Town, USA 91234

For ____________ ____________

Reading Supermarket Receipts

Materials

- actual supermarket receipts, one for every two students
- page 218, reproduced on an overhead transparency

Steps to Follow

1. Show some actual supermarket receipts and ask students to identify what you are holding. Explain that when you check out at the supermarket, the clerk hands you a cash register tape that lists the names of the items you purchased, their prices, and your total cost. This tape is called a receipt.

2. Show the transparency of a sample receipt (page 218). Locate the following information:

   - store name
   - location
   - date of purchase
   - time of purchase
   - names of items bought
   - cost
   - tax paid
   - total cost of all items purchased

3. Examine how produce is listed on a receipt—the weight and the cost per pound are given and then the item and price are listed on the next line.

4. Divide students into pairs and give each pair an actual grocery receipt.

5. Instruct students to find the same information on their receipt. Ask the following questions:

   Is any of the information different?
   Are there additional types of information?

Authentic Reading Practice, Grades 1–3 • EMC 3300

Comparison Shopping

```
                2% MILK
                CHIPS                    3.09
    2.90 LB @ .39/LB                     2.09
    WT      BANANAS
            GREEN ONIONS                 1.13
            SLICED TURKEY                 .67
            CUCUMBERS                    1.99
    4.01 LB @ .49/LB                      .39
    WT      ORANGES
            ROMA TOMATO                  1.96
            ROMAINE LETTUCE               .25
            BABY CARROTS                  .69
    @ 2/5.00                             1.19
            SPAGHETTI SAUCE
    2.06 LB @ 3 LB/.99                   2.50
    WT      RED POTATOES
    3.83 LB @ .25/LB                      .68
    WT      SEEDLESS WATERMELON
                                          .96
            WHOLE WHEAT BREAD            1.69
            INSTANT OATMEAL             1.49
            96 OZ ORANGE JUICE          2.99
    3.75 LB @ 1.29/LB
    WT      CHICKEN THIGHS               4.84

            TAX                          .00

            BALANCE DUE                 28.60
            CASH                        40.00

            CHANGE                      11.40



                7/25/01 11:27

            Thank you for shopping
               at HillTop Grocery
            3000 Murray Hill Road
             Hometown, U.S.A.
```

Supermarket Extras

Put reading at the supermarket skills to work by having students shop in the class minimarket and solve "supermarket stumpers."

ACTIVITIES

A Classroom Minimarket (Pages 220 and 221)
Your students will learn so much when they shop in their own minimarket.

Supermarket Stumpers (Pages 222–224)
Set aside an area to post a supermarket stumper for the class to solve. Challenge students to solve the problems independently by a given time. Spend time discussing different ways that the problem was solved. Reproduce the form on page 224 to provide blank stumper cards so that students may develop their own supermarket stumpers to share with the class.

A Classroom Minimarket

Involve your students in the planning and setup of your market, as well as the operations of it.

Materials

- display shelves or tables
- checkout table or desk
- bulletin board or easel to post signage
- food and miscellaneous items (empty containers or full) found in a supermarket
- baskets with handles for shopping
- paper or plastic bags for carrying items away
- play money
- checks on page 216, reproduced
- envelopes
- adding machine or calculator
- receipts
- stickers for prices
- construction paper or posterboard for signs
- marking pens
- apron for checker

Preparing the Minimarket

1. With the class, choose a name for your store and decide on its hours of operation.

2. Assign students to make the store sign and "open hours" sign.

3. Price the items. You might start with even amounts, such as $2.00 or 40¢ to make it easier for shoppers to keep track of the amount of their purchases.

4. Choose students to stock the shelves. They will need to decide how the items are to be categorized and make signs for the various sections.

5. Discuss the various roles students can play at the minimarket—stockers, cashier, courtesy clerk, and shoppers.

6. Decide on how the roles are to be rotated so that each student gets a chance to experience each role. Develop a chart that assigns students to various roles at a particular time.

7. Sort the money into sets of varying amounts and place it in envelopes. Put some money (both bills and coins) in a container for the cashier to make change.

8. Cut apart checks and place them in an envelope or a folder.

Shopping at the Minimarket

1. Model the process several times, guiding students through the roles as the rest of the class observes.
  - The shopper takes an envelope of money or a check (you might designate certain days as "cash only" days and other days as "check" days).
  - Shopper counts the money to get an idea of how much may be spent.
  - Shopper chooses the items, placing them in his or her shopping basket. Along the way, the shopper should attempt to keep track of the amount being spent.
  - Shopper takes the basket to the checkout table.
  - Checker reads the prices and enters them on the adding machine or calculator as the courtesy clerk bags the items.
  - Checker announces the total, and the shopper counts out the correct amount of money or writes a check.
  - Checker presents the shopper with a receipt.

2. Shopper deposits his or her grocery bags at a predetermined place, to be "reshelved" later by the stockers.

3. When you feel your students are ready, let them go to the center on their own.

Note: Reproduce this page and page 223 to use with "Supermarket Stumpers" on page 219.

Supermarket Stumper 1

Dirk's mom wanted some green beans from the supermarket. Dirk found them in three different sections. Tell the names of the sections where Dirk might have found them. Write a question that Dirk could ask his mother to find out which beans to choose.

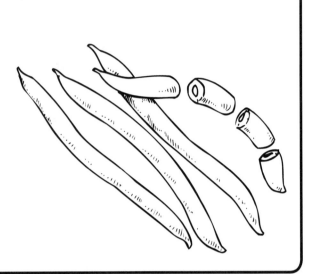

Supermarket Stumper 2

The soups in the supermarket display are arranged in alphabetical order. Show the order that these soups would be in on the shelf:

tomato soup

cream of celery

bean and bacon

beef and barley

chicken noodle

vegetable

cream of mushroom

New England clam chowder

Supermarket Stumper 3

The new stocker needs to restock the shelves. Match the product with the section where it belongs.

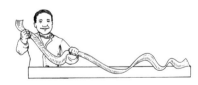

paper towels

canned peaches

Saltines® crackers

frozen peas

French bread

• bakery goods

• paper products

• frozen foods

• cookies and crackers

• canned fruits and vegetables

Supermarket Stumper 4

Mel, the manager of the produce section at the supermarket, wants a sign to advertise a special on a new crop of cantaloupes. The cantaloupes will sell for 39 cents a pound. They usually sell for 99 cents a pound. Design an advertisement for this special. Include all the information that the consumer needs to know.

Supermarket Stumper 5

Tiffany wants to buy the ingredients for a batch of cupcakes. She has a boxed cake mix with these instructions:

1. Heat oven to 350° F. Grease pan with shortening; lightly flour.
2. Mix cake mix, 1¼ cups water, ¼ cup oil, and 2 eggs.
3. Pour into cupcake pans. Bake 25 minutes.

Write a shopping list for the other things that she needs.

Supermarket Stumper 6

The customer service representative has three unhappy customers. Tell what you would do to help each one.

• The milk that Mr. Brown bought is sour.

• The eggs in Mrs. White's grocery bag were cracked when the bag broke on the way to her car.

• Tommy can't find the hamburger buns.

Note: Reproduce these forms for students to make their own Supermarket Stumpers. (See page 219.)

Supermarket Stumper

____

____

____

By ______________________

Supermarket Stumper

____

____

____

By ______________________

Supermarket Stumper

____

____

____

By ______________________

Reading at the Supermarket Skills Checklist ✓

	Students' Names									
Writes about experiences in a supermarket logbook										
Reads signage outside the market										
Reads a supermarket directory to locate an item										
Locates a desired item in the store										
Reads the names of common supermarket items										
Categorizes items based on similarities										
Can name the major sections of a supermarket and the types of products found there										
Reads and uses a shopping list										
Makes a shopping list to get the ingredients for a recipe										
Reads information on a coupon										
Reads supermarket ads and compares prices										
Can read a check										
Writes a check with guidance										
Reads a supermarket receipt										

Part 5

Reading for Information

As students become more competent readers, they will begin to do more reading outside of "reading time" at school. In this section, students will practice reading various types of everyday-life materials to find information.

Reading Nonfiction Books

This section contains activities to help students discover the differences between fiction and nonfiction books, learn how to use each section of a nonfiction book, and develop strategies for locating information.

ACTIVITIES

What Is a Nonfiction Book? (Page 228)

Explain that some books tell us a story (fiction), while others give us information (nonfiction). Show several books, one at a time. Read the titles and a few pages of each. After each book ask, "Do you think this is a fiction book or a nonfiction book?" Discuss how students decided on their answers.

Explain that most nonfiction books have several parts that help us find information. Reproduce page 228 on an overhead transparency. Point to each book part on the chart and give its name and then show the parts in an actual book.

A Sample Nonfiction Book (Pages 229–242)

Reproduce or make transparencies of the sample book pages and activity sheets (pages 232–242). Use the teaching guide on pages 229–231 to present the information. Take every opportunity to practice using the parts of a nonfiction book in real-life experiences across the curriculum.

Note: Make a transparency of this page to use with "What Is a Nonfiction Book?" on page 227.

The Parts of a Nonfiction Book

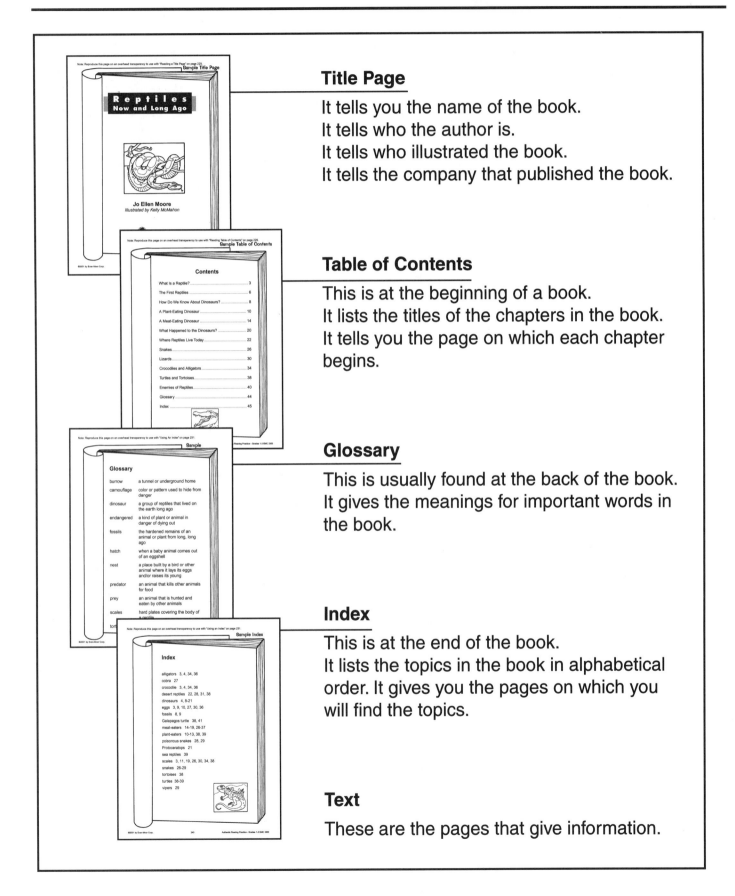

Title Page

It tells you the name of the book.
It tells who the author is.
It tells who illustrated the book.
It tells the company that published the book.

Table of Contents

This is at the beginning of a book.
It lists the titles of the chapters in the book.
It tells you the page on which each chapter begins.

Glossary

This is usually found at the back of the book.
It gives the meanings for important words in the book.

Index

This is at the end of the book.
It lists the topics in the book in alphabetical order. It gives you the pages on which you will find the topics.

Text

These are the pages that give information.

A Sample Nonfiction Book

Materials
- pages 232, 233, 235, 236, 238, 240, reproduced on overhead transparencies
- pages 234–237, 239, 241, 242, reproduced for individual students
- a selection of nonfiction books containing the various features to be studied (see below)

Reading a Title Page
1. Show the transparency of page 232.
2. Ask students to name the title, author, illustrator, and publisher.
3. Give a nonfiction book to each pair of students. Instruct them to locate the title page and find the items discussed on the transparency.

Reading a Table of Contents
1. Show the transparency of page 233.
2. If necessary, explain what the term *contents* means.
3. Read the transparency together.
4. Give the name of a chapter and ask students to find the page number it begins on. Give a page number and have students name the chapter.
5. Complete the worksheet on page 234 as a group or independently.
6. Have students locate the tables of contents in nonfiction books. More capable students may formulate questions to ask other students.

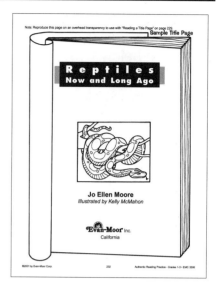

Reading the Text

Use the transparencies and individual copies of pages 235 and 236 to practice the strategies given below.

After completing all five strategies, have students complete page 237 as a review.

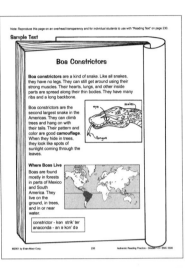

1. Using Headings

Explain how the headings give us a clue as to what will be in the paragraphs that follow. Read each heading, discuss what students think they will find, and then read the paragraph to locate facts.

2. Looking for Important Words

Discuss what kind of words you might look for. In this chapter about a boa constrictor, you might look for words that lead you to information about what it eats, where it lives, what it looks like, etc.

Explain that key words can be found in several ways. Sometimes they are a part of the title or headings. Sometimes they are words that have been printed in a different way (bold or italics). Have students skim through the pages to find words or phrases that have been highlighted in some manner. Read these together and discuss how these words can help us find information. For example, the word **camouflage** is in bold. If we are looking for information about how a snake protects itself, this bolded word leads us quickly to the correct paragraph.

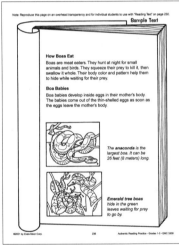

3. Using Graphics

Look at the map, illustrations, and diagram to see what additional information can be found. Read the captions together for more information.

4. Using Pronunciation Guides

Use the pronunciation key in the box to sound out new words.

5. Pre-questioning

Develop a set of three or four questions to ask students to think about as they are reading the text. Write the questions on the chalkboard. This pre-questioning prepares students to recognize important information as they are reading. These may be general questions that can be used with any animal, such as:

  What does it look like?
  Where does it live?
  What does it eat?
  How does it raise its young?

Or they can be specific to the piece your students will be reading:

  What does a boa constrictor look like?
  How does it capture its food?
  Why does it have a pattern on its scales?

Using a Glossary

1. Show the transparency of page 238.

2. Ask questions such as:

How is the page arranged? (alphabetical order)
What kinds of information does the page provide?
(gives words and their meanings)

3. Give a word and ask students to find and read its meaning.

4. Develop a definition of *glossary*. (A glossary is a section of a book that gives the meanings of important words used in the book.)

5. Complete the worksheet on page 239 as a group or individually.

Using an Index

1. Show the transparency of page 240.

2. Ask questions such as:

How is the page arranged? (alphabetical order)
What kinds of information does the page provide?
(lists topics that are found in the book and gives the page numbers where each topic can be found)

3. Give a topic and have students tell on which pages information on that topic would be found.

4. Complete the worksheet on page 241 as a group or individually.

Reviewing Parts of a Nonfiction Book

1. Give each student or pair of students a nonfiction book and a copy of page 242.

2. Students use the form to report on the parts of the book.

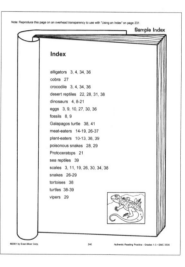

Note: Make a transparency of this page to use with "Reading a Title Page" on page 229.

Sample Title Page

Reptiles
Now and Long Ago

Jo Ellen Moore
Illustrated by Kelly McMahon

Evan-Moor Inc.
California

Note: Make a transparency of this page to use with "Reading a Table of Contents" on page 229.

Sample Table of Contents

Contents

Note: Reproduce this page for students to use with "Reading a Table of Contents" on page 229.

Name:

Table of Contents

Where would you look to find the answers to these questions?

To find the answer to this question:	I would look in the chapter that begins on page:

1. What is a reptile?

_____

2. What is the name of one plant-eating dinosaur?

_____

3. Do lizards lay eggs?

_____

4. How are turtles and tortoises different?

_____

5. Why aren't there any dinosaurs living today?

_____

6. What were the first reptiles like?

_____

7. How did meat eaters catch their food?

_____

8. How is a crocodile different from an alligator?

_____

 Authentic Reading Practice, Grades 1–3 • EMC 3300

Sample Text

Boa Constrictors

Boa constrictors are a kind of snake. Like all snakes, they have no legs. They can still get around using their strong muscles. Their hearts, lungs, and other inside parts are spread along their thin bodies. They have many ribs and a long backbone.

Boa constrictors are the second largest snake in the Americas. They can climb trees and hang on with their tails. Their pattern and color are good **camouflage**. When they hide in trees, they look like spots of sunlight coming through the leaves.

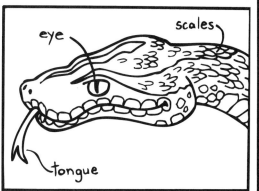

Where Boas Live

Boas are found mostly in forests in parts of Mexico and South America. They live on the ground, in trees, and in or near water.

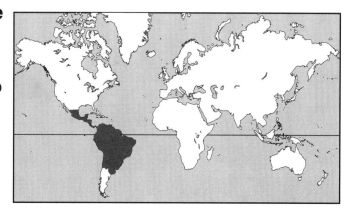

constrictor - kən strik´ ter
anaconda - an ə kon´ də

How Boas Eat

Boas are meat eaters. They hunt at night for small animals and birds. They squeeze their prey to kill it, then swallow it whole. Their body color and pattern help them to hide while waiting for their prey.

Boa Babies

Boa babies develop inside eggs in their mother's body. The babies come out of the thin-shelled eggs as soon as the eggs leave the mother's body.

*The **anaconda** is the largest boa. It can be 26 feet (8 meters) long.*

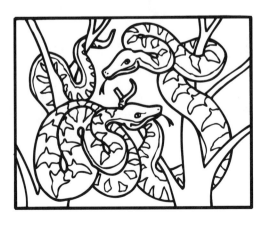

***Emerald tree boas** hide in the green leaves waiting for prey to go by.*

Authentic Reading Practice, Grades 1–3 • EMC 3300

Name:

Boa Constrictors

1. What kind of animal is a boa
   constrictor?

   _____

2. Name three places in the forest
   you might see a boa
   constrictor.

   a. _____

   b. _____

   c. _____

3. How do boa constrictors kill
   their food?

   _____

4. Label the parts of this snake.

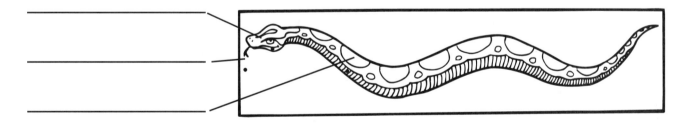

5. Color in this map to show
   where boa constrictors
   are found.

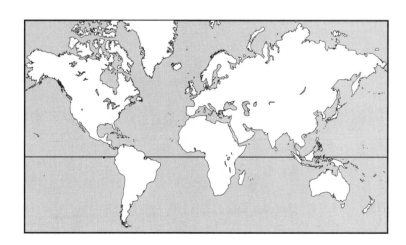

Sample

Glossary

burrow	a tunnel or an underground home
camouflage	a color or pattern used to hide from danger
dinosaur	a group of reptiles that lived on the earth long ago
endangered	a kind of plant or animal in danger of dying out
fossils	the hardened remains of an animal or a plant from long, long ago
hatch	when a baby animal comes out of its eggshell
nest	a place built by a bird or other animal where it lays its eggs and/or raises its young
predator	an animal that kills other animals for food
prey	an animal that is hunted and eaten by other animals
scales	hard plates covering the body of a reptile
tortoise	a land turtle

Note: Reproduce this page for individual students to use with "Using a Glossary" on page 231.

Name:

Glossary

Use the glossary to answer these questions.

1. How is a nest used?

____

____

2. What does a predator do?

____

____

3. What happens when something hatches?

____

____

4. How is camouflage useful?

____

____

5. What is a tortoise?

____

____

6. What is a burrow used for?

____

____

Note: Make a transparency of this page to use with "Using an Index" on page 231.

Index

alligators   3, 4, 34, 36

cobras   27

crocodiles   3, 4, 34, 36

desert reptiles   22, 28, 31, 38

dinosaurs   4, 8–21

eggs   3, 9, 10, 27, 30, 36

fossils   8, 9

Galápagos turtles   38, 41

meat eaters   14–19, 26–37

plant eaters   10–13, 38, 39

poisonous snakes   28, 29

Protoceratops   21

sea reptiles   39

scales   3, 11, 19, 26, 30, 34, 38

snakes   26–29

tortoises   38

turtles   38, 39

vipers   29

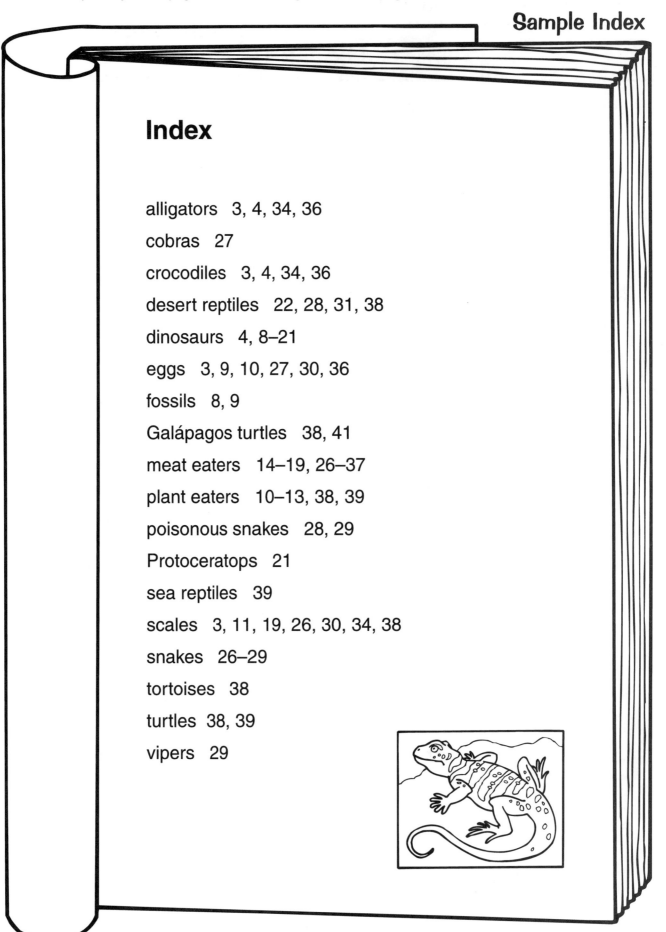

Authentic Reading Practice, Grades 1–3 • EMC 3300

Name:

Index Worksheet

Read the index to find the answers.   **Yes** or **No**

1. Will you find out about eggs on page 30?   _____

2. Will you find out about reptiles in the desert on pages 28 and 38?   _____

3. Will you find out about meat eaters on pages 10–13?   _____

4. Can you read about alligators and crocodiles on the same pages?   _____

Read the index to find the answers.

1. On what page can you read about vipers?   _____

2. On what pages can you read about rattlesnakes?   _____

3. On how many pages can you read about eggs? _____

4. Are there more pages that tell about scales or about alligators?   _____

Note: Reproduce this page for individual students to use with "Reviewing Parts of a Nonfiction Book" on page 231.

Name:

My Report About ____________________
title of the book

1. This book had: **Yes** or **No**

a table of contents ________

an index ________

a glossary ________

2. Look at the title page. Write the author's name.

____

3. Name two things in the table of contents. Tell the page numbers.

a. ____________________

b. ____________________

4. Here is a new word I read in the glossary: ____________________

It means ____________________

____

5. Name two things in the index. Tell the page numbers.

a. ____________________

b. ____________________

Reading Charts and Diagrams

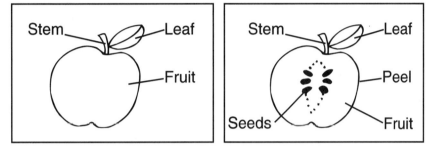

Charts and diagrams are used in nonfiction and reference books to present additional information on the subject. This section contains sample charts and diagrams to use for practice. Find opportunities to read charts and diagrams that naturally occur as parts of units of study.

ACTIVITIES

Life Cycle of a Butterfly (Pages 244 and 245)
Make an overhead transparency of page 244; reproduce page 245 for individual students. Show the transparency. Ask, "What does this diagram show us? What information can you find by reading it?" Ask specific questions that require students to read the diagram for information. Have students answer the questions about the diagram on page 245.

Parts of a Snail (Pages 246 and 247)
Make an overhead transparency of page 246; reproduce page 247 for individual students. Show the transparency. Ask, "What does this diagram show us? What information can you find by reading it?" Ask specific questions that require students to read the diagram for information. Have students answer the questions about the diagram on page 247.

Life Cycle of a Butterfly

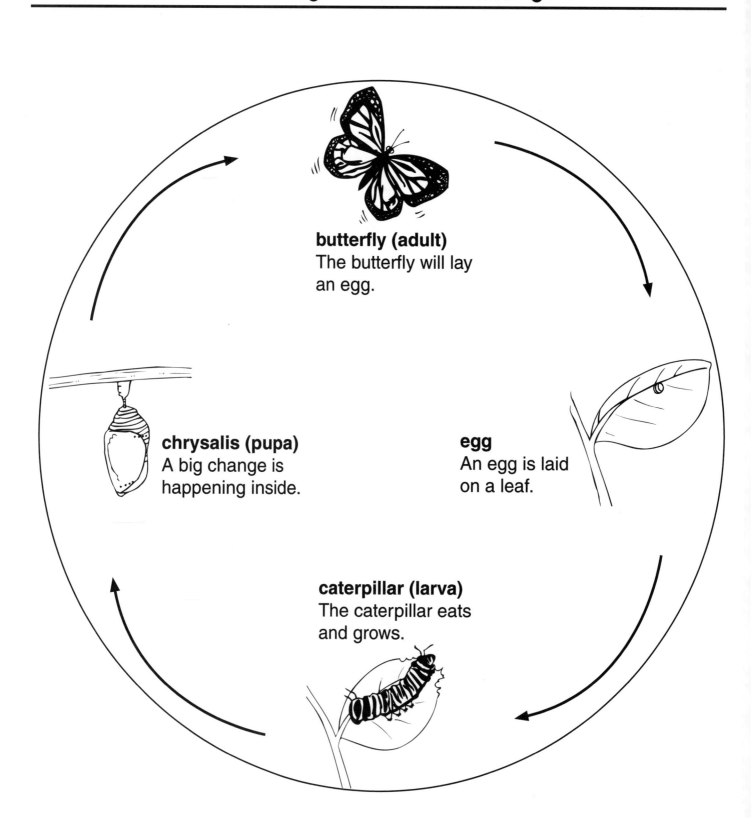

butterfly (adult)
The butterfly will lay
an egg.

chrysalis (pupa)
A big change is
happening inside.

egg
An egg is laid
on a leaf.

caterpillar (larva)
The caterpillar eats
and grows.

                   Authentic Reading Practice, Grades 1–3 • EMC 3300

Name:

Life Cycle of a Butterfly

This chart shows the stages in the life of a butterfly.

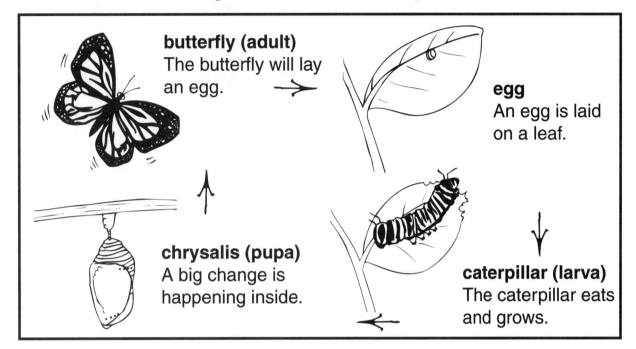

butterfly (adult)
The butterfly will lay an egg.

egg
An egg is laid on a leaf.

chrysalis (pupa)
A big change is happening inside.

caterpillar (larva)
The caterpillar eats and grows.

Look at the chart. Answer the questions.

1. Where is the egg laid?

_____

2. What happens inside the chrysalis?

_____

3. What does the caterpillar do all day?

_____

Write in your own words how a butterfly grows.

_____

_____

_____

Note: Make a transparency of this page to use with "Parts of a Snail" on page 243.

Parts of a Snail

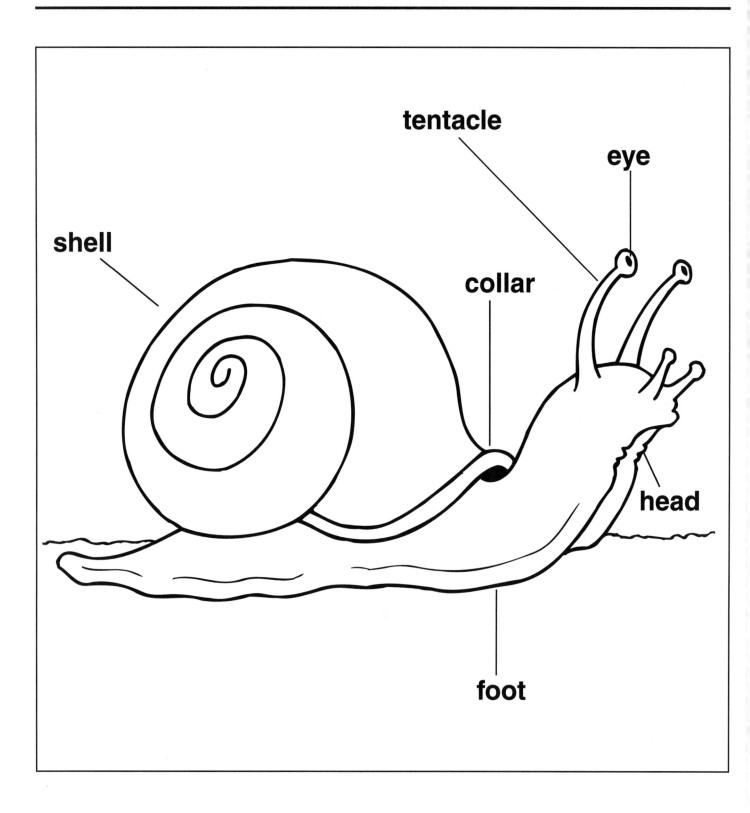

Name:

Parts of a Snail

This diagram shows the parts of the body of a snail.

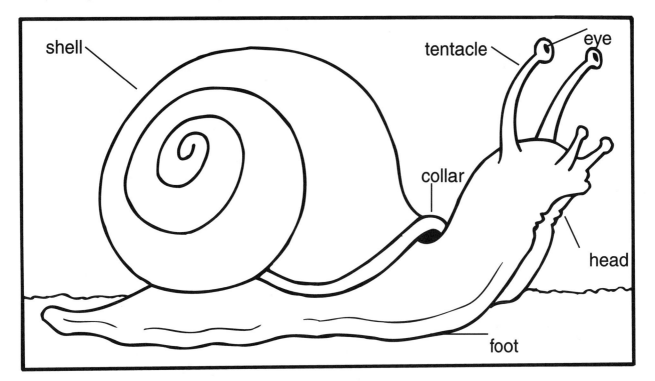

Look at the diagram. Answer the questions.

1. What is the hard covering of the snail called?

_____

2. What is the part a snail crawls on called?

_____

3. Where are the eyes of a snail?

_____

4. How many pairs of tentacles does a snail have?

_____

Reading Dictionaries

This chapter provides students with practice in putting words in alphabetical order, locating words in a dictionary, and understanding the parts of a dictionary entry.

ACTIVITIES

Alphabetical Order (Pages 249 and 250)
Reproduce these pages for students to practice putting words in alphabetical order.

Finding Letters in the Dictionary (Page 251)
The first step in learning to look up a word is to have an idea about in which part of the dictionary words certain letters are likely to be found.

Finding Words in the Dictionary (Pages 252–254)
Students begin to use guide words to locate entry words in a dictionary.

Finding Word Meanings (Pages 255 and 256)
Use the transparency you made for the previous lesson to help students learn about entries in a dictionary.

Name:

Word Search

Pat and Herbie need to know the meaning of some words they are going to use in a report about animals. Put their words in alphabetical order to make it easier to find them in a dictionary.

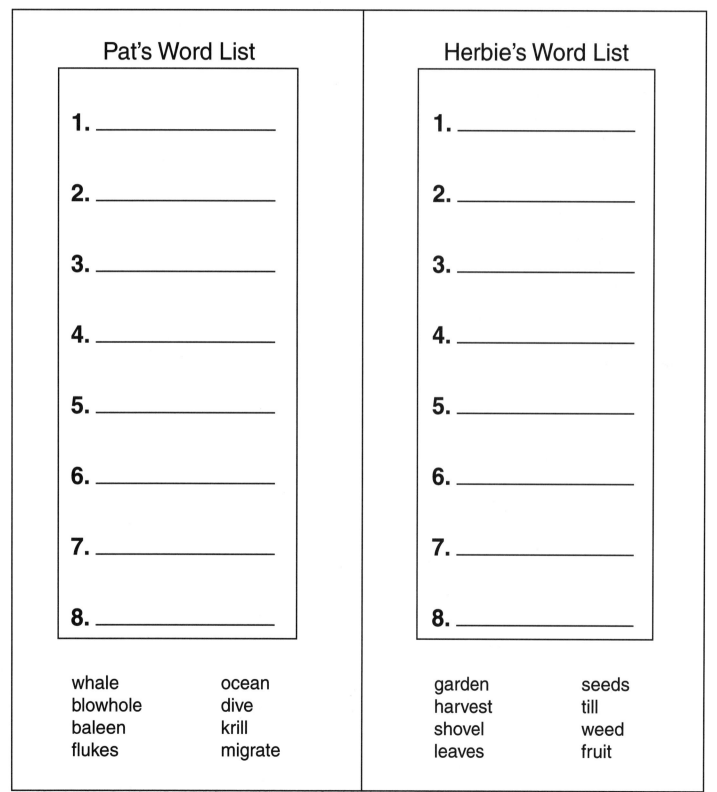

Pat's Word List

1. _____

2. _____

3. _____

4. _____

5. _____

6. _____

7. _____

8. _____

Herbie's Word List

1. _____

2. _____

3. _____

4. _____

5. _____

6. _____

7. _____

8. _____

whale	ocean
blowhole	dive
baleen	krill
flukes	migrate

garden	seeds
harvest	till
shovel	weed
leaves	fruit

What Comes Next?

Circle the word that would come next in the dictionary.

1. | bat | bug   box   bell

2. | watch | window   wolf   whale

3. | jelly | joke   jacket   jingle

4. | cake | comb   chicken   cube

5. | zebra | zoom   zipper   zap

6. | fish | flower   fast   feather

7. | rake | rose   ring   rug

8. | pickle | poster   package   pretty

Finding Letters in the Dictionary

Materials
• an appropriate dictionary, at least one for every two or three students

Steps to Follow

1. Ask several students to find the "g" section of the dictionary. Have the rest of the class observe how long it takes these students to find the letter. Explain that there is a strategy that can help them locate letters more quickly.

2. On the chalkboard, write the letters of the alphabet divided into sets as shown:

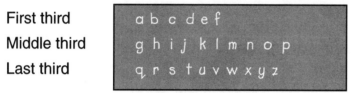

First third	a b c d e f
Middle third	g h i j k l m n o p
Last third	q r s t u v w x y z

3. Ask students to name a letter from one of those sections. Model how you would find it by dividing the dictionary roughly into thirds.

> *I am looking at the edge of the dictionary and thinking about how I would divide the pages into three parts that are close to the same size. I'll put my fingers here and here. That looks like three pretty equal parts to me. According to our list, the letter "k" is in the middle third. It looks like it's about in the middle of that section. So I will put my finger in the middle of that section and open the dictionary. Wow, look at that! I opened to a page with "k" words on it.*

4. Pass out dictionaries and have students locate letters using the "thirds" method.

Finding Words in the Dictionary

Materials
- page 253, reproduced on an overhead transparency
- page 254, reproduced for individual students
- dictionaries
- large index cards or rectangular-shaped tagboard
- marking pen

Steps to Follow

1. In advance, make a master list of pairs of guide words from your dictionary and several words found on those pages. Include several words that begin with the same letter, but are not found on that page. Write the entry words on cards.

2. Show the transparency. Point out the guide words at the top of the page, tell what they are called, and explain that these words help to find a word more quickly. Ask, "Do you see the guide words anywhere else on the page?" Show that these are the first and last words on the page. Explain that all words on the page will be in alphabetical order between the two guide words.

3. Read the entry words together. Underline the first two letters in each entry word to see if the words are in the correct order.

4. Pass out dictionaries. Give a page number. Have students find that page and read the guide words. Repeat this for several pages in the dictionary.

5. Write a pair of guide words from your master list on the chalkboard. Pass out the words cards.

6. Have each student read his or her card. If the word would come between the guide words, the student sets the card in the chalk tray. After every word has been placed in the tray, have the class explain why the word would be (or would not be, in the event of mistakes) on that dictionary page.

7. Have students complete page 254 for additional practice in finding words in the dictionary.

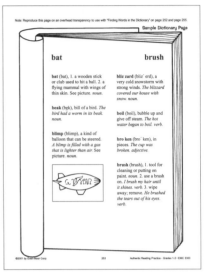

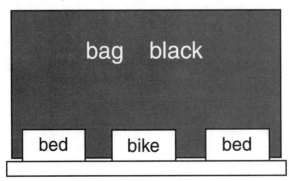

Sample Dictionary Page

bat   brush

bat (bat), **1.** a wooden stick or club used to hit a ball. **2.** a flying mammal with wings of thin skin. *noun.*

beak (bēk), the bill of a bird. *The bird had a worm in its beak. noun.*

blimp (blimp), a kind of balloon that can be steered. *A blimp is filled with a gas that is lighter than air. See picture. noun.*

bliz zard (blizʹ erd), a very cold snowstorm with strong winds. *The blizzard covered our house with snow. noun.*

boil (boil), bubble up and give off steam. *The hot water began to boil. verb.*

bro ken (broʹ ken), in pieces. *The cup was broken. adjective.*

brush (brush), **1.** a tool for cleaning or putting on paint. *noun.* **2.** use a brush on. *I brush my hair until it shines. verb.* **3.** wipe away; remove. *He brushed the tears out of his eyes. verb.*

Name:

Find It in the Dictionary

Find the word:	Is it in the dictionary? **Yes** or **No**	What page is it on?
bat	_____	_____
globe	_____	_____
lava	_____	_____
snake	_____	_____
yak	_____	_____
zip	_____	_____
doll	_____	_____
mango	_____	_____

Finding Word Meanings

Materials

- page 253, reproduced on an overhead transparency
- page 256, reproduced for individual students after writing in words that can be found in your class dictionaries
- dictionaries

Steps to Follow

1. Show the transparency of the sample dictionary page.

2. Ask these questions:

Are there any words on this page that have more than one meaning? (*bat, brush*)

How can you tell? (each meaning is numbered)

What is given to make the meaning of a word clearer? (sentence, picture)

3. Write two words on the chalkboard that can be found on a page of your dictionary. Read the meaning of one of the words. Students are to find each word and determine which one has the meaning given.

4. Have students use dictionaries to find the meanings of the words reproduced on page 256. They should write the first meaning given.

Name:

What Does It Mean?

Find these words: Tell what they mean.

1. _____   _____
                                  _____

2. _____   _____
                                  _____

3. _____   _____
                                  _____

4. _____   _____
                                  _____

5. _____   _____
                                  _____

6. _____   _____
                                  _____

Reading Encyclopedias

While encyclopedias are generally difficult for young readers to use, you can begin to help them understand how to use them and the types of information they might find in them.

ACTIVITIES

Introducing Encyclopedias (Pages 258 and 259)
This lesson will help students understand how encyclopedias' topics are organized in alphabetical order.

Finding a Topic in an Encyclopedia (Pages 260 and 261)
Once students have selected the correct volume of an encyclopedia, they need to understand how to use the words at the top of the page to locate the topic.

A Sample Encyclopedia Article (Pages 262–267)
Teaching ideas and sample encyclopedia pages help students practice information-gathering strategies.

Introducing Encyclopedias

Materials
- page 259, reproduced for individual students
- set of encyclopedias

Steps to Follow

1. Hold up any volume of your set of encyclopedias and read the letter or letters on the spine. Point out that some letters are on more than one volume and that some volumes have more than one letter.

2. Explain that all the topics in a volume begin with the letter or letters on the spine. Point out that people are listed by their last names. Ask students to tell which volume their name would be in if they were listed in the encyclopedia.

3. Have the class say the letters of the alphabet in order. As each letter is named, have that volume returned to the shelf.

4. Have students complete page 259 for practice in using the alphabet to find the correct volume.

Note: Reproduce this page to use with "Introducing Encyclopedias" on page 258.

Name:

The Encyclopedia

Directions: List the entries below next to the correct letter of the encyclopedia.

A _____   L _____

B _____   M _____

DE _____   XYZ _____

apples	Michigan	x-ray
baboon	dinosaur	Johann S. Bach
electricity	Abraham Lincoln	Louisiana
zebra	mushroom	Asia

©2001 by Evan-Moor Corp.   259   Authentic Reading Practice - Grades 1-3 • EMC 3300

Name: _____

The Encyclopedia

List the entries in the box below next to the correct letter of the encyclopedia.

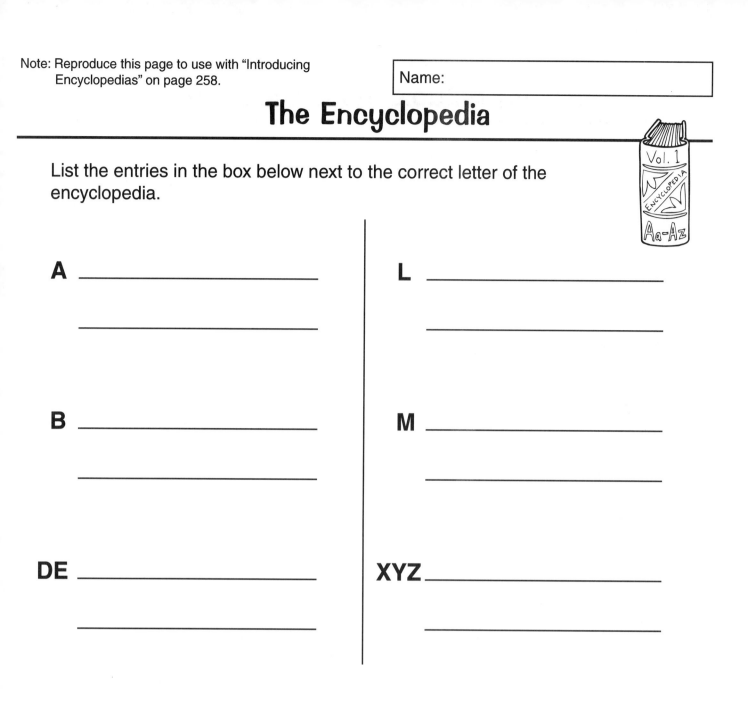

A _____

_____

B _____

_____

DE _____

_____

L _____

_____

M _____

XYZ _____

_____

apples	Michigan	x-ray
baboon	dinosaur	Johann S. Bach
electricity	Abraham Lincoln	Louisiana
zebra	mushroom	Asia

Finding a Topic in an Encyclopedia

Materials
- page 261, reproduced and cut in half so that each group receives one half
- set of encyclopedias
- index cards on which you have written a topic from each volume (see step 3)
- numbered index cards on which you have written three or more topics (don't duplicate volumes on the cards) (see step 6)

Note: Reproduce this form to use with "Finding a Topic in an Encyclopedia" on page 260.

Card # _____

Topic   Volume   Page

_____ _____ _____
_____ _____ _____
_____ _____ _____

Steps to Follow

1. Select one volume of the encyclopedia. Open it to various places and read the words you find at the top of each page. Point out that this topic (or topics) will be found on the page. Explain that sometimes there will be other topics on the page. These will come alphabetically between the topics listed at the top of the page.

2. Divide the class into six groups. Give each group one volume of the encyclopedia.

3. Give each group a card with a topic from that volume to locate.

4. Have each group raise their hands when they have located their topic.

5. Have groups exchange topic cards and encyclopedia volumes, looking for the new topic.

6. Give each group an index card with three or more topics written on it and half of page 261. Groups are to determine in which volume each topic on their list can be found. They then locate the topic and write the volume and page number on which the topic was found.

         Authentic Reading Practice, Grades 1–3 • EMC 3300

Note: Reproduce this form to use with "Finding a Topic in an Encyclopedia" on page 260.

Card # _____

Topic	Volume	Page
_____	_____	_____
_____	_____	_____
_____	_____	_____

- -

Card # _____

Topic	Volume	Page
_____	_____	_____
_____	_____	_____
_____	_____	_____

A Sample Encyclopedia Article

Use the sample article on cats to teach students about the various parts of an encyclopedia article and how to glean information using several different strategies. You may want to conduct each part of the lesson at a separate time to maximize retention of the strategies presented.

Materials
- page 264, reproduced on an overhead transparency and for individual students
- page 266, reproduced on an overhead transparency
- pages 265 and 267, reproduced for individual students

Gaining Information from Headings

1. Show the transparency of page 264 and/or provide students with individual copies of the sample article.

2. Ask students to name the parts of the article—title, headings, pictures, or diagrams.

3. Refer to the headings and ask questions such as:

   Who remembers what a heading is?
   (title of a part of a story or article)

   How do headings help you when you read for information?
   (you can quickly find the section that has the specific information you are looking for)

   What are the headings in this article on cats?

   What are some things you might find out in the section "Care of the Cat"?
   　Would you learn what to feed a cat?
   　Would you learn how much cats weigh?

   What do you think you might learn in (name other sections of the article)?

4. Ask students to suggest other headings they might find if this article were to continue. (Origin of the Species, A History of Domestic Cats, Breeds of Cats, Showing and Judging Cats, Cat in Myths and Folklore, Cat Diseases, Cats in Art, etc.)

Gaining Information Using Pictures and Designs

1. Show the transparency of page 264 and/or provide students with individual copies of the sample article.

2. Ask students to name the pictures and diagrams in the article—Parts of a Cat, Short-haired Cat, Long-haired Cat.

3. Ask, "Which of these is a diagram?" (Parts of a Cat) and "How do you know?" (the parts are labeled)

4. Refer to the diagram and ask questions such as:

> What can you learn by studying the diagram? (what the parts of a cat's head are called)

> Where is a cat's muzzle? (the part of the head where the nose and mouth are located)

> Where do cats have whiskers besides near their noses? (above the eyes)

> Why do you think diagrams are found in encyclopedia articles? (to show things that would be hard to explain in words)

5. Have students complete page 265 to practice reading and labeling diagrams.

Using Key Words to Gain Information

1. Write "Key Words" on the chalkboard. Tell the class, "It is easier to find information to answer questions if you think about important or key words. You do not have to read every word in the article. Instead, you look for the key word as if you were looking for a word in a word search puzzle.

"For example, if I want to know what cats do when they wake up, I would look for the words 'wake up' in the article. Let's see if we can find the words 'wake up' in our article on cats."

2. Show the transparency of the sample article. Allow time for students to scan for the words "wake up" and raise their hands when they have located the words. Ask, "What do cats do when they wake up?" (stretch their bodies)

3. Show the transparency of page 266, "Questions about Cats." Give each student a copy of the sample article on page 264.

4. Ask students to help you fill in the heading they would look under and the key words they would look for. Find the answer to each question by using headings and key words. Discuss how well the strategies worked.

Reading an Entire Article

1. As a class or individually, read the entire article on cats.

2. Answer the true/false statements on page 267.

3. Discuss whether it was easier to read the whole article after having studied the headings and pictures.

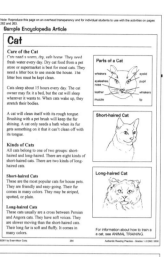

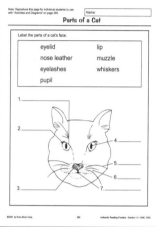

Sample Encyclopedia Article

Cat

Care of the Cat

Cats need a warm, dry, safe home. They need fresh water every day. Dry cat food from a pet store or supermarket is best for most cats. They need a litter box to use inside the house. The litter box must be kept clean.

Cats sleep about 15 hours every day. The cat owner may fix it a bed, but the cat will sleep wherever it wants to. When cats wake up, they stretch their bodies.

A cat will clean itself with its rough tongue. Brushing with a pet brush will keep the fur shiny. A cat needs a bath only when its fur gets something on it that it can't clean off with its tongue.

Kinds of Cats

All cats belong to one of two groups: short-haired and long-haired. There are eight kinds of short-haired cats. There are two kinds of long-haired cats.

Short-haired Cats

These are the most popular cats for house pets. They are friendly and easy-going. Their fur comes in many colors. They may be striped, spotted, or plain.

Long-haired Cats

These cats usually are a cross between Persian and Angora cats. They have soft voices. They are slower moving than the short-haired cats. Their long fur is soft and fluffy. It comes in many colors.

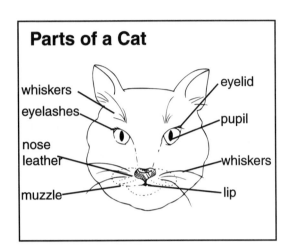

Parts of a Cat

whiskers · eyelashes · nose leather · muzzle · eyelid · pupil · whiskers · lip

Short-haired Cat

Long-haired Cat

For information about how to train a a cat, see ANIMAL TRAINING.

Note: Reproduce this page for individual students to use with "Gaining Information Using Pictures and Designs" on page 262.

Name:

Parts of a Cat

Label the parts of a cat's face.

eyelid	lip
nose leather	muzzle
eyelashes	whiskers
pupil	

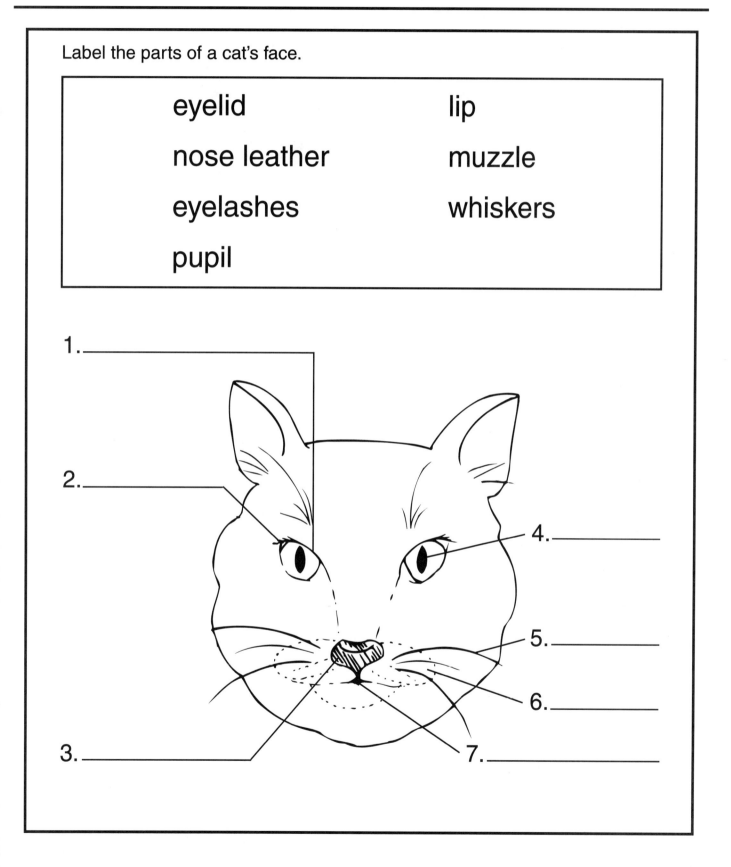

1. _____

2. _____

4. _____

5. _____

6. _____

3. _____

7. _____

Authentic Reading Practice, Grades 1–3 • EMC 3300

Questions About Cats

	Heading	Key Words
Why are short-haired cats so popular?		
What kind of food is best for your cat?		
How many groups of cats are there?		
How does a cat clean itself?		
What is the fur of long-haired cats like?		
How much do cats sleep?		
When should you give your cat a bath?		

Name:

Facts About Cats

Make an **X** under the correct answer.	True	False
1. Scraps from the dinner table are the best food for pet cats.		
2. A cat cleans itself with its rough tongue.		
3. All cats belong to the same group.		
4. Angora cats are noisy.		
5. Cats can only live inside a house.		
6. You should give your cat a bath every week.		
7. Cats with short hair make good pets.		
8. Brushing will keep a cat's fur shiny.		

Reading Magazines

There are marvelous magazines for children being published today. The lessons and activities in this chapter will help students become familiar with the parts of a magazine, thus increasing their abilities to enjoy these periodicals.

ACTIVITIES

Magazines for a Primary Classroom (Page 269)
Review names and addresses of some of the magazines appropriate for primary students.

What's in a Magazine? (Pages 270 and 271)
Students explore children's magazines to see what they contain.

Reading Magazine Covers (Pages 272 and 273)
Use a sample magazine cover to explore the elements found on most magazine covers.

Reading a Magazine Table of Contents (Pages 274 and 275)
Use a sample table of contents to learn about the elements found there.

Reading Magazine Advertisements (Pages 276 and 277)
Look at a sample advertisement and talk about what ads are trying to accomplish.

Reading a Magazine Article (Pages 278–283)
Read a sample magazine article on chimpanzees to practice using headings, captions, maps, and diagrams to gain information.

Magazines for a Primary Classroom

There are many fine magazines for children. Here is a partial list of the many excellent children's magazines appropriate for the primary grades. Some focus on a particular subject area; others are eclectic.

1. Cobblestone Publications
   (A division of the *Cricket Magazine* Group)
   www.cobblestonepub.com
   • *Appleseeds* (grades 2–4) (general, social studies)
   • *Click* (grades 1–2) (science, nature, history, technology)

2. *Lady Bug* (grades PreK–1) and *Spider* (grades 1–4) (literary)
   Cricket Magazine Group
   www.cricketmag.com

3. *My Big Backyard* and *Ranger Rick*
   National Wildlife Federation
   1-800-611-1599

4. *Kids Discover* (grades 3 and up)
   1-800-825-2821

5. *Chickadee* (puzzles, games, animal features, fiction)
   1-800-551-6957

6. *Highlights*
   www.highlights.com

What's in a Magazine?

cover	IIII I
table of contents	IIII I
articles about people, places, and things	IIII II
making things	IIII
stories and poems	III
riddles and puzzles	III
advertisements	IIII
illustrations	IIII
photographs	II
maps	I

Note: Reproduce this page to use with "What's in a Magazine" on page 270.

Name:

Magazine Review

name of the magazine   date

1. List three articles in this magazine.

_____

_____

2. Is there a place to read letters from readers?

3. On what page will you find riddles or puzzles?

4. Is there a poster you can pull out?

5. Is there a poem in this magazine?

What is the poem's title?

What page is it on?

6. Write the name of one article you would like to read. What page is it on?

Evan-Moor Corp.   271   Authentic Reading Practice · Grades 1–3 · EMC 3300

Materials
- a selection of children's magazines, two per group
- chart paper
- marking pen
- page 271, reproduced for individual students

Steps to Follow

1. Hold up a selection of magazines. Ask questions such as:
    What magazines do you read?
    Where do you get the magazines you read?
    Can you think of a magazine that tells about people? places? animals? sports?

2. List the magazines students name. Make a class tally to determine favorites and graph the information.

3. Divide the class into small groups. Give each group a magazine. Instruct groups to look through the magazines to find the different types of sections they contain.

4. Have each group tell one thing they found in their magazine. (Explain that they may not repeat what another group says.) Write each part mentioned on a chart. Continue until no group can offer new information.

5. Ask, "Do all magazines have these same parts?" Name each section listed on the chart one at a time. Tally how many groups find that part in their magazine.

6. When finished, ask, "What did we find in **all** the magazines?"

7. Give each group a new magazine. Give each student a copy of page 271. Students work together to answer the questions, with each student responsible for completing the worksheet.

Note: Reproduce this page to use with "What's in a Magazine?" on page 270.

Name:

Magazine Review

name of the magazine | date

1. List three articles in this magazine.

2. Is there a place to read letters from readers?

3. On what page will you find riddles or puzzles?

4. Is there a poster you can pull out?

5. Is there a poem in this magazine?

What is the poem's title?

What page is it on?

6. Write the name of one article you would like to read. What page is it on?

Reading Magazine Covers

A magazine's cover is the feature that attracts readers. Publishers put large amounts of time and resources into cover design. In this activity, students will learn about the information found on magazine covers.

Materials
- overhead transparency of page 273
- real magazines
- chart paper
- marking pen

Steps to Follow

1. View the transparency of the sample cover and ask questions such as:

   What is the name of the magazine?

   What kinds of articles are in this issue?

   Is there a contest of some kind? What could you win?

   What does the cover have that makes you want to read the issue?

   What other information is found on the cover?

2. On a chart, list the standard information one might find on a magazine cover— name of magazine, publication date, price, announcement of a contest, titles of feature articles, photographs or illustrations.

3. Divide students into small groups and give each group several magazines. They are to examine the cover of each magazine to see if they can find each of the cover items listed on the chart.

4. While students are examining their magazines, add two columns entitled "Yes" and "No" to the chart.

5. Tally the cover features groups found in their magazines.

Sample Magazine Cover

Exploring Our World

June 2001

Watching Chimpanzees

Super Contest!

WIN a trip to the RAINFOREST!

Have you met an Okapi?

6 Pages of Fun!

Reading a Magazine Table of Contents

Materials
- overhead transparency of page 275
- children's magazines or photocopies of several tables of contents

Steps to Follow

1. Show the transparency of the sample table of contents. If necessary, discuss what a *table of contents* is. Ask, "Where else are tables of contents found?"

2. Ask questions such as:

   On what page does the article on chimpanzees begin?

   Where would you look if you wanted to find out more about riding in a kayak?

   Are there any stories or poems in this issue? What are they called?

   What kinds of fun pages are in this magazine?

3. Point out that the page also contains other information. Ask students to read the rest of the page (or read it to them). Then have students explain what other kinds of information they found.

4. Supply each pair of students with a children's magazine or photocopied table of contents.

5. Partners read their table of contents together and talk about the items they locate.

6. Select a pair of students to tell something they found in their table of contents. (titles of stories or poems, game pages, pictures, explanation of the cover, etc.) Ask how many other pairs found a similar item. Continue until no new items are named.

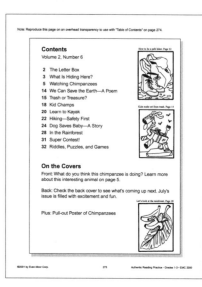

Note: Make a transparency of this page to use with "Reading a Magazine" on page 274.

Contents
Volume 2, Number 6

How to be a safe hiker. Page 22

Kids make art from trash. Page 15

On the Covers

Front: What do you think this chimpanzee is doing? Learn more about this interesting animal on page 5.

Back: Check the back cover to see what's coming up next. July's issue is filled with excitement and fun.

Plus: Pull-out Poster of Chimpanzees

Let's look at the rainforest. Page 28

Authentic Reading Practice, Grades 1–3 • EMC 3300

Reading Magazine Advertisements

Although most children's magazines that you find in a school setting contain no advertising, many "newsstand" children's magazines do.

Materials
• assortment of child-appropriate magazine ads
• overhead transparency of page 277

Steps to Follow

1. Show several advertisements. Explain that companies that make the products pay the magazine to publish their ads. This is one of the ways the magazine makes money. Ask:

   Why do you think companies put ads in magazines?

   Have you or members of your family ever bought something that you saw in a magazine advertisement?

2. View the transparency of the sample ad. Discuss how words and pictures are used to try to sell the product. Ask questions such as:

   What is this advertisement trying to sell you?

   What words tell what is special about this bike?

   Why do you think the advertisement says "Be a part of the adventure?"

   What does the advertisement say you will get free?

   Do you have to do anything to get the free helmet?

   Discuss what the phrases "with purchase" and "at participating stores" mean.

3. Divide students into small groups and give each group several ads. Instruct groups to list all the words used to make someone want to buy the product.

4. Compile a class list of powerful advertising words.

Note: Make a transparency of this page to use with "Reading Magazine Advertisements" on page 276.

Reading a Magazine Article

Materials

- sample article on pages 280–282, reproduced on overhead transparencies (Optional: reproduce copies for individual students)
- page 283, reproduced on a transparency and for individual students
- assortment of children's magazines

Explain to students that magazines do certain things to make it easier for readers to find information. List these "reader helpers" on the chalkboard and discuss them one at a time using the sample article:

- headings
- captions
- key words
- maps, charts, and diagrams
- sidebars (boxed inserts)

Headings

1. Show the transparency of page 280. Ask, "What is the title of this magazine article? What do you think you are going to learn about when you read the article?"

2. Point to the first heading "Life Among the Trees." Tell students, "This is called a *heading*. It is like a title for this part of the story. What do you think this short part of the story will be about?"

3. Repeat step 2 for the other headings on that page and pages 281 and 282.

4. Ask specific questions on the article and have students tell in what section they would look for the information. Read that section to determine if the answer is there. For example:

> Which part of the article would tell about different sounds and calls chimpanzees make?

> Where would you find out how many chimps live together in a group?

> If you wanted to know if chimpanzees are an endangered species, which part would tell you?

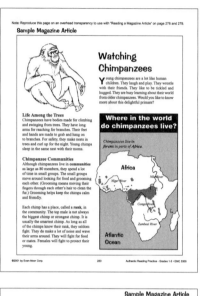

Captions

1. Explain that *captions* are the words under a picture, map, or diagram, etc. Frequently captions contain important facts.

2. Read the captions in the sample article and discuss the information contained.

Key Words

1. Explain that magazines may use bold or a different kind of type for important words. We call these *key words*.

2. Have students find these key words in the sample article. Ask specific questions and have students tell which key word might help them locate the answer to each question.

Maps and Diagrams

Study the map of Africa on page 280 and the chart showing sizes of various apes on page 281. Ask what information is presented in each.

Sidebars

1. Show the transparency of page 282. Explain to students that a *sidebar* is a section of information separated from the main article and usually enclosed in a box or a shaded area. A sidebar gives extra information that does not really fit in the article.

2. Ask students to locate the sidebars on page 282. Read the titles of both and the caption under the illustration.

Read the Article

1. Read the entire article together.

2. Give each student a copy of the questions on page 283.

3. Read each question together. Determine the key words in each question. Next, locate the heading under which you are likely to find those key words. Read that section as a group or individually.

4. Have students raise their hands when the answer to the question is read.

5. Discuss the answer and agree on wording. Write the answer on the transparency as students write on their worksheets.

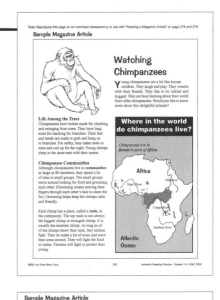

Sample Magazine Article

Watching Chimpanzees

Young chimpanzees are a lot like human children. They laugh and play. They wrestle with their friends. They like to be tickled and hugged. They are busy learning about their world from older chimpanzees. Would you like to know more about this delightful primate?

Life Among the Trees

Chimpanzees have bodies made for climbing and swinging from trees. They have long arms for reaching for branches. Their feet and hands are made to grab and hang on to branches. For safety, they make nests in trees and curl up for the night. Young chimps sleep in the same nest with their moms.

Chimpanzee Communities

Although chimpanzees live in **communities** as large as 80 members, they spend a lot of time in small groups. The small groups move around looking for food and grooming each other. (Grooming means moving their fingers through each other's hair to clean the fur.) Grooming helps keep the chimps calm and friendly.

Each chimp has a place, called a **rank**, in the community. The top male is not always the biggest chimp or strongest chimp. It is usually the smartest chimp. As long as all of the chimps know their rank, they seldom fight. They do make a lot of noise and wave their arms around. They will fight for food or mates. Females will fight to protect their young.

Where in the world do chimpanzees live?

Chimpanzees live in **forests** *in parts of* **Africa**.

Africa

Nile River

Niger River

Congo River

Zambezi River

Atlantic Ocean

Apes come in various sizes...

from the tiny lemur to the large gorilla. The chimpanzee is one of the larger apes.

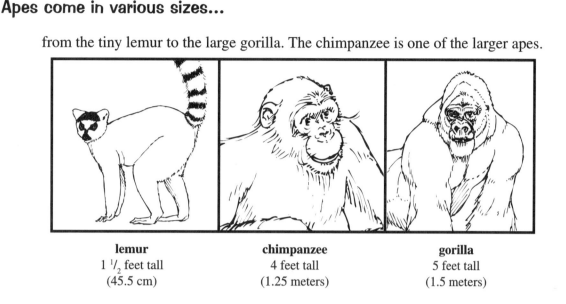

lemur	**chimpanzee**	**gorilla**
1 $\frac{1}{2}$ feet tall	4 feet tall	5 feet tall
(45.5 cm)	(1.25 meters)	(1.5 meters)

Can chimps talk?

Can you tell how your friends are feeling just by looking at their faces? Chimpanzees cannot speak the way we do. But they can **communicate**. They use their whole bodies to let other chimps know what they feel. When they are scared, they will hold hands or hug. They show friendship by hugging and kissing when they meet. A chimp will put out a hand to beg for food from another chimp.

They also use different calls to mean different things. They use calls to warn others of danger. They also use calls that mean they are happy or not happy.

What does a hungry chimp eat?

Chimpanzees usually eat fruit and leaves. They will also eat eggs and insects. They will sometimes hunt other animals for meat.

Chimps know how to use twigs as **tools** for finding food. They take the leaves off the twig and poke it into a termite nest or a beehive. They eat the insects or the honey that sticks to the twig.

 Authentic Reading Practice, Grades 1–3 • EMC 3300

Sample Magazine Article

Rock-a-Bye Baby Chimp

Chimpanzees in the wild are good mothers. Chimpanzees are **mammals**. Like all mammals, baby chimpanzees drink their mother's milk. Young chimps stay with their mothers for many years. Chimps take a long time to grow up (about 5 years). They have a lot to learn about taking care of themselves. They learn how to find food, build nests, avoid danger, and fight by watching and playing with other chimps.

Danger! Danger!

Chimpanzees are in **danger of disappearing** in the wild. There used to be millions of them; now there are fewer than 150,000.

Chimps are killed by people and animals. They are hunted to sell to zoos, circuses, and labs. Their forest homes are being destroyed to build farms, villages, and roads.

It is important to try to find ways to save the chimps that still live in the wild. There need to be safe **parks** and **reserves** where they can live.

The Jane Goodall Institute works to save wild chimpanzees and to make people more aware of environmental problems. To find out more about this organization and how you can join, donate, or become a chimpanzee guardian, go to the JGI Website: www.janegoodall.org

Do you know her name?

Jane Goodall studied the chimpanzees of Gombe for thirty years. Her careful notes and observations helped scientists around the world have a better understanding of animal behavior.

Note: Make a transparency of this page and copies for students to use with "Read the Article" on page 279.

Name:

Watching Chimpanzees

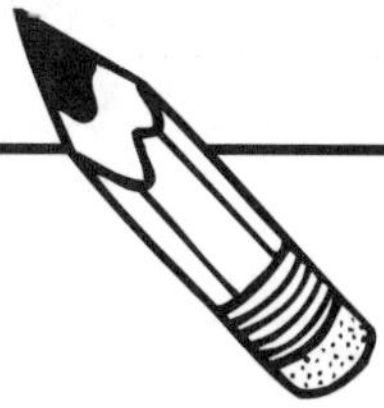

Read the article and answer these questions.

1. Where do chimpanzees live?

____

2. How do we know chimpanzees are good mothers?

____

____

3. How do chimpanzees "talk" to each other?

____

____

4. Why are chimpanzees in danger?

____

____

5. Who is Jane Goodall?

____

6. What kinds of tools do chimpanzees use?

____

Reading for Information Skills Checklist ✓

	Students' Names									
Distinguishes a nonfiction book from a fiction book										
Identifies the parts of a nonfiction book										
Uses a table of contents, glossary, and an index										
Uses key words to locate information										
Gathers information from charts and diagrams										
Alphabetizes words to the second letter										
Uses "section" strategy to locate letters in a dictionary										
Uses guide words to locate words in a dictionary										
Reads dictionary entries to determine the meanings of words										
Understands how topics are organized in an encyclopedia										
Can locate a given topic in an encyclopedia										
Reads a sample encyclopedia article using headings, key words, pictures, and diagrams to locate information										
Names the features generally found in magazines										
Reads a magazine cover and identifies its features										
Can use a magazine table of contents										
Understands the aspects of magazine advertisements										
Reads a sample magazine article using headings, key words, pictures, and diagrams to locate information										

Answer Key

Page 4

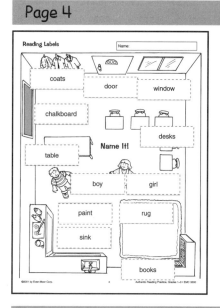

Page 62

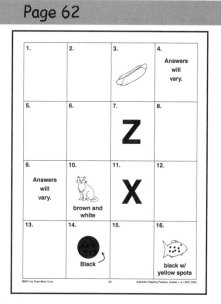

Page 63

Page 64

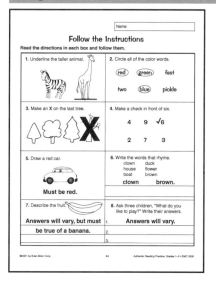

Page 145

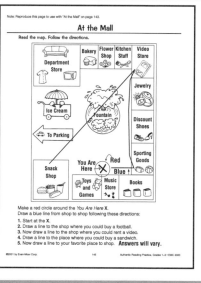

Page 147

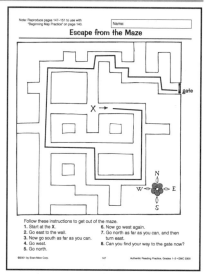

Page 148

Page 149

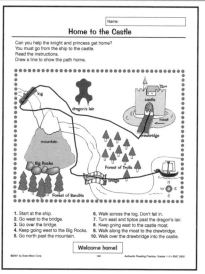

Page 150

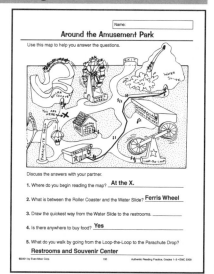

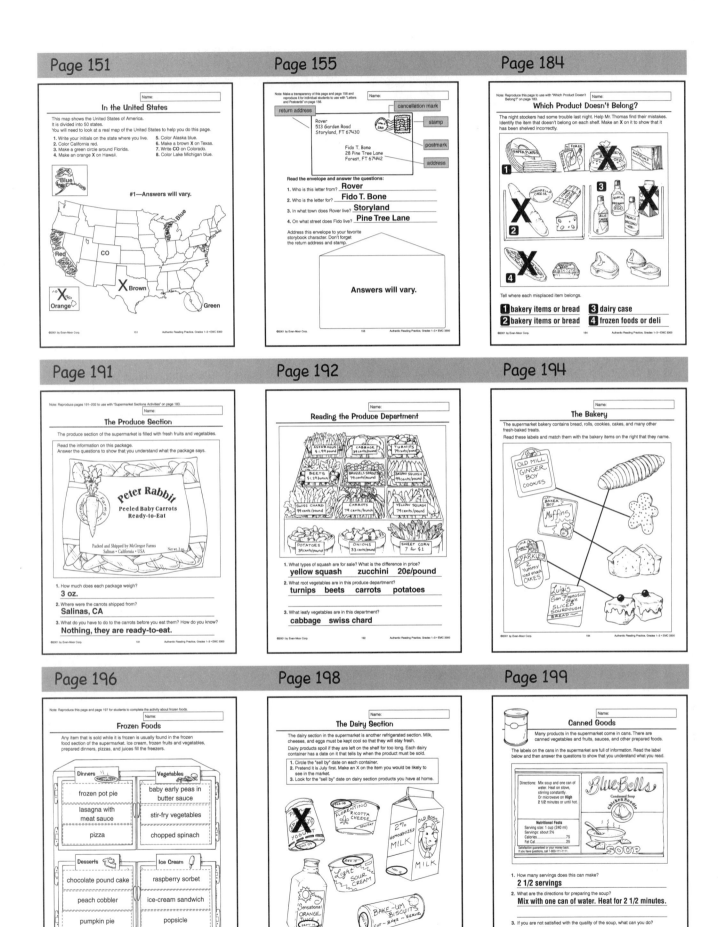

Page 151

In the United States

This map shows the United States of America.
It is divided into 50 states.
You will need to look at a real map of the United States to help you do this page.

1. Write your initials on the state where you live.
2. Color California red.
3. Make a green circle around Florida.
4. Make an orange X on Hawaii.
5. Color Alaska blue.
6. Make a brown X on Texas.
7. Write CO on Colorado.
8. Color Lake Michigan blue.

#1—Answers will vary.

Page 155

Note: Make a transparency of this page and page 156 and reproduce it for individual students to use with "Letters and Postcards" on page 156.

Rover
513 Garden Road
Storyland, FT 67430

Fido T. Bone
28 Pine Tree Lane
Forest, FT 67442

Read the envelope and answer the questions:

1. Who is this letter from? **Rover**
2. Who is the letter for? **Fido T. Bone**
3. In what town does Rover live? **Storyland**
4. On what street does Fido live? **Pine Tree Lane**

Address this envelope to your favorite storybook character. Don't forget the return address and stamp.

Answers will vary.

Page 184

Note: Reproduce this page to use with "Which Product Doesn't Belong?" on page 183.

Which Product Doesn't Belong?

The night stockers had some trouble last night. Help Mr. Thomas find their mistakes. Identify the item that doesn't belong on each shelf. Make an X on it to show that it has been shelved incorrectly.

Tell where each misplaced item belongs.

1 **bakery items or bread**   3 **dairy case**
2 **bakery items or bread**   4 **frozen foods or deli**

Page 191

Note: Reproduce pages 191–202 to use with "Supermarket Sections Activities" on page 183.

The Produce Section

The produce section of the supermarket is filled with fresh fruits and vegetables.

Read the information on this package.
Answer the questions to show that you understand what the package says.

Peter Rabbit Peeled Baby Carrots Ready-to-Eat
Packed and Shipped by McGregor Farms Salinas • California • USA   Net wt. 3 oz.

1. How much does each package weigh?
3 oz.
2. Where were the carrots shipped from?
Salinas, CA
3. What do you have to do to the carrots before you eat them? How do you know?
Nothing, they are ready-to-eat.

Page 192

Reading the Produce Department

1. What types of squash are for sale? What is the difference in price?
yellow squash   zucchini   20¢/pound
2. What root vegetables are in this produce department?
turnips   beets   carrots   potatoes
3. What leafy vegetables are in this department?
cabbage   swiss chard

Page 194

The Bakery

The supermarket bakery contains bread, rolls, cookies, cakes, and many other fresh-baked treats.

Read these labels and match them with the bakery items on the right that they name.

Page 196

Note: Reproduce this page and page 197 for students to complete the activity about frozen foods.

Frozen Foods

Any item that is sold while it is frozen is usually found in the frozen food section of the supermarket. Ice cream, frozen fruits and vegetables, prepared dinners, pizzas, and juices fill the freezers.

Dinners
frozen pot pie
lasagna with meat sauce
pizza

Vegetables
baby early peas in butter sauce
stir-fry vegetables
chopped spinach

Desserts
chocolate pound cake
peach cobbler
pumpkin pie

Ice Cream
raspberry sorbet
ice-cream sandwich
popsicle

Page 198

The Dairy Section

The dairy section in the supermarket is another refrigerated section. Milk, cheeses, and eggs are kept cool so that they will stay fresh.

Dairy products spoil if they are left on the shelf for too long. Each dairy container has a date on it that tells by when the product must be sold.

1. Circle the "sell by" date on each container.
2. Pretend it is July first. Make an X on the item you would be likely to see in the market.
3. Look for the "sell by" date on dairy section products you have at home.

Page 199

Canned Goods

Many products in the supermarket come in cans. There are canned vegetables and fruits, sauces, and other prepared foods.

The labels on the cans in the supermarket are full of information. Read the label below and then answer the questions to show that you understand what you read.

1. How many servings does this can make?
2 1/2 servings
2. What are the directions for preparing the soup?
Mix with one can of water. Heat for 2 1/2 minutes.
3. If you are not satisfied with the quality of the soup, what can you do?
Call 1-800-111-1111

Authentic Reading Practice, Grades 1–3 • EMC 3300

Page 204

Name: _____

Which Shopping List?

Cut out each list below and paste it beside the picture that shows those items.

loaf of bread	eggs
milk	orange juice
cottage cheese	bananas
jam	milk
cookies	strawberries

can of soup	loaf of bread
chips	can of tuna
chicken	lettuce
apple	flour
honey	nuts

Page 234

Name: _____

Table of Contents

Where would you look to find the answers to these questions?

To find the answer to this question:	I would look in the chapter that begins on page:
1. What is a reptile?	3
2. What is the name of one plant-eating dinosaur?	10
3. Do lizards lay eggs?	30
4. How are turtles and tortoises different?	38
5. Why aren't there any dinosaurs living today?	20
6. What were the first reptiles like?	6
7. How did meat eaters catch their food?	14
8. How is a crocodile different from an alligator?	34

Page 237

Name: _____

Boa Constrictors

1. What kind of animal is a boa constrictor? **a snake**

2. Name three places in the forest you might see a boa constrictor.
   a. **on the ground**
   b. **in trees**
   c. **near water**

3. How do boa constrictors kill their food? **squeeze prey**

4. Label the parts of this snake.

eye
tongue
scales

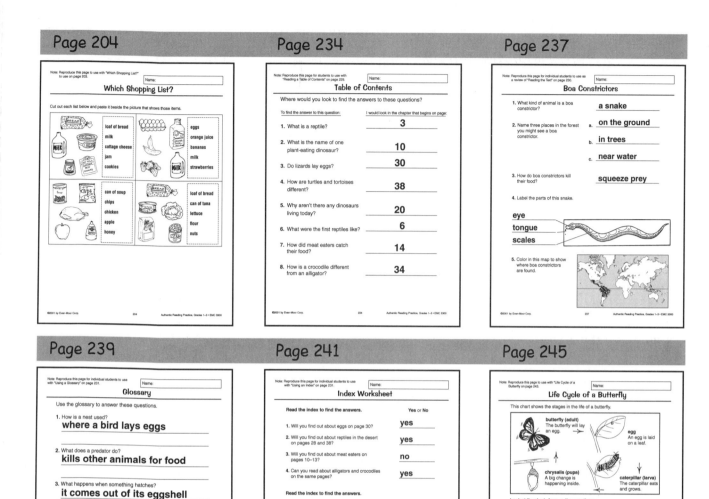

5. Color in this map to show where boa constrictors are found.

Page 239

Name: _____

Glossary

Use the glossary to answer these questions.

1. How is a nest used? **where a bird lays eggs**

2. What does a predator do? **kills other animals for food**

3. What happens when something hatches? **it comes out of its eggshell**

4. How is camouflage useful? **to hide from danger**

5. What is a tortoise? **a land turtle**

6. What is a burrow used for? **it is an underground home**

Page 241

Name: _____

Index Worksheet

Read the index to find the answers. **Yes or No**

1. Will you find out about eggs on page 30? **yes**
2. Will you find out about reptiles in the desert on pages 28 and 38? **yes**
3. Will you find out about meat eaters on pages 10–13? **no**
4. Can you read about alligators and crocodiles on the same pages? **yes**

Read the index to find the answers.

1. On what page can you read about vipers? **29**
2. On what pages can you read about rattlesnakes? **26—29**
3. On how many pages can you read about eggs? **6 pages**
4. Are there more pages that tell about scales or about alligators? **scales**

Page 245

Name: _____

Life Cycle of a Butterfly

This chart shows the stages in the life of a butterfly.

butterfly (adult) The butterfly will lay an egg.
egg An egg is laid on a leaf.
chrysalis (pupa) A big change is happening inside.
caterpillar (larva) The caterpillar eats and grows.

Look at the chart. Answer the questions.

1. Where is the egg laid? **on a leaf**
2. What happens inside the chrysalis? **a change happens**
3. What does the caterpillar do all day? **eats and grows**

Write in your own words how a butterfly grows.
Answers will vary, but must include: an egg is laid, a caterpillar hatches; it eats and grows; inside a chrysalis the caterpillar changes into a butterfly.

Page 247

Name: _____

Parts of a Snail

This diagram shows the parts of the body of a snail.

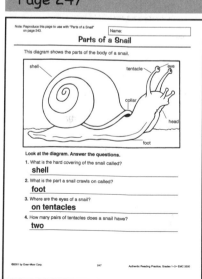

shell
tentacle
eye
collar
head
foot

Look at the diagram. Answer the questions.

1. What is the hard covering of the snail called? **shell**
2. What is the part a snail crawls on called? **foot**
3. Where are the eyes of a snail? **on tentacles**
4. How many pairs of tentacles does a snail have? **two**

Page 249

Name: _____

Word Search

Pat and Herbie need to know the meaning of some words they are going to use in a report about animals. Put their words in alphabetical order to make it easier to find them in a dictionary.

Pat's Word List	Herbie's Word List
1. **baleen**	1. **fruit**
2. **blowhole**	2. **garden**
3. **dive**	3. **harvest**
4. **flukes**	4. **leaves**
5. **krill**	5. **seeds**
6. **migrate**	6. **shovel**
7. **ocean**	7. **till**
8. **whale**	8. **weed**

whale	ocean	garden	seeds
blowhole	dive	harvest	till
baleen	krill	shovel	weed
flukes	migrate	leaves	fruit

Page 250

Name: _____

What Comes Next?

Circle the word that would come next in the dictionary.

1.	bat	bug	box	(bell)
2.	watch	window	wolf	(whale)
3.	jelly	joke	jacket	(jingle)
4.	cake	comb	(chicken)	cube
5.	zebra	zoom	(zipper)	zap
6.	fish	(flower)	fast	feather
7.	rake	rose	(ring)	rug
8.	pickle	(poster)	package	pretty

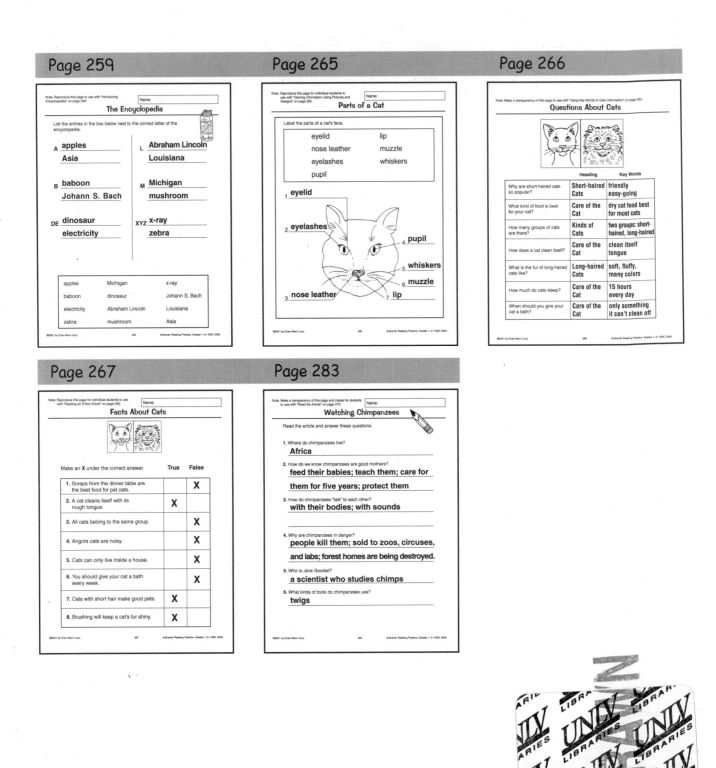

Page 259

Note: Reproduce this page to use with "Introducing Encyclopedias" on page 258.

Name: _____

The Encyclopedia

List the entries in the box below next to the correct letter of the encyclopedia.

A apples
   Asia

B baboon
   Johann S. Bach

DE dinosaur
    electricity

L Abraham Lincoln
   Louisiana

M Michigan
   mushroom

XYZ x-ray
     zebra

apples	Michigan	x-ray
baboon	dinosaur	Johann S. Bach
electricity	Abraham Lincoln	Louisiana
zebra	mushroom	Asia

©2001 by Evan-Moor Corp.   259   Authentic Reading Practice, Grades 1–3 • EMC 3300

Page 265

Note: Reproduce this page for individual students to use with "Gaining Information Using Pictures and Designs" on page 262.

Name: _____

Parts of a Cat

Label the parts of a cat's face.

eyelid	lip
nose leather	muzzle
eyelashes	whiskers
pupil	

1. eyelid
2. eyelashes
3. nose leather
4. pupil
5. whiskers
6. muzzle
7. lip

©2001 by Evan-Moor Corp.   265   Authentic Reading Practice, Grades 1–3 • EMC 3300

Page 266

Note: Make a transparency of this page to use with "Using Key Words to Gain Information" on page 263.

Questions About Cats

	Heading	Key Words
Why are short-haired cats so popular?	Short-haired Cats	friendly easy-going
What kind of food is best for your cat?	Care of the Cat	dry cat food best for most cats
How many groups of cats are there?	Kinds of Cats	two groups: short-haired, long-haired
How does a cat clean itself?	Care of the Cat	clean itself tongue
What is the fur of long-haired cats like?	Long-haired Cats	soft, fluffy, many colors
How much do cats sleep?	Care of the Cat	15 hours every day
When should you give your cat a bath?	Care of the Cat	only something it can't clean off

©2001 by Evan-Moor Corp.   266   Authentic Reading Practice, Grades 1–3 • EMC 3300

Page 267

Note: Reproduce this page for individual students to use with "Reading an Entire Article" on page 263.

Name: _____

Facts About Cats

Make an **X** under the correct answer.

	True	False
1. Scraps from the dinner table are the best food for pet cats.		X
2. A cat cleans itself with its rough tongue.	X	
3. All cats belong to the same group.		X
4. Angora cats are noisy.		X
5. Cats can only live inside a house.		X
6. You should give your cat a bath every week.		X
7. Cats with short hair make good pets.	X	
8. Brushing will keep a cat's fur shiny.	X	

©2001 by Evan-Moor Corp.   267   Authentic Reading Practice, Grades 1–3 • EMC 3300

Page 283

Note: Make a transparency of this page and copies for students to use with "Read the Article" on page 279.

Name: _____

Watching Chimpanzees

Read the article and answer these questions.

1. Where do chimpanzees live?
   Africa

2. How do we know chimpanzees are good mothers?
   feed their babies; teach them; care for them for five years; protect them

3. How do chimpanzees "talk" to each other?
   with their bodies; with sounds

4. Why are chimpanzees in danger?
   people kill them; sold to zoos, circuses, and labs; forest homes are being destroyed.

5. Who is Jane Goodall?
   a scientist who studies chimps

6. What kinds of tools do chimpanzees use?
   twigs

©2001 by Evan-Moor Corp.   283   Authentic Reading Practice, Grades 1–3 • EMC 3300